Automated Threat Handbook
Web Applications

The *OWASP Automated Threat Handbook* provides actionable information and resources to help defend against automated threats to web applications

Authors

Colin Watson and Tin Zaw

Project Reviewers

Igor Andriushchenko, Gabriel Mendez Justiniano and Matt Tesauro

Other Project Contributors

Jason Chan, Mark Hall, Andrew van der Stock and Roland Weber, everyone else who contributed information anonymously, and the authors of the referenced information sources; v1.2: Sumit Agarwal and Omri Iluz

Version 1.2 published 15th February 2018

ISBN 978-1-329-42709-9

© 2015-2018 OWASP Foundation

This document is licensed under the Creative Commons Attribution-ShareAlike 3.0 license

Contents

Prefaces 1

Terminology 4

Introduction 5

Research 7

The Ontology 9

    Figure 1: Threat Events, ordered by ascending name 10

    Figure 2: Subset related to Account Credentials 11

    Figure 3: Subset related to Payment Cardholder Data 11

    Figure 4: Subset related to Vulnerability Identification 11

    Figure 5: Subset related to Availability of Inventory 11

    Figure 6: WASC Threat Classification view of the Threat Events 12

    Figure 7: Mitre CAPEC view of the Threat Events 13

Countermeasures 19

    Figure 8: Automated Threat Countermeasure Classes 20

Use Case Scenarios 23

Project Details 26

Handbook Roadmap 27

Automated Threat Event Reference 28

Preface to v1.2

From its original release in 2015, the *OWASP Automated Threat Handbook* has now become a de facto industry standard in detecting and mitigating threats by malicious web automation. Every bot mitigation vendor and many buyers of these services now use the ontology defined in this handbook. In this new version of the OWASP Automated Threat Handbook , the previously named automated threat event OAT-009 CAPTCHA Bypass has been renamed **OAT-009 CAPTCHA Defeat**, and a new threat event **OAT-021 Denial of Inventory** has been added.

CAPTCHA Bypass was originally used for OAT-009 since this is by far the most common name used. However, subsequent feedback suggests this is confusing, since the puzzle is not actually bypassed, but is solved in an automated manner – not because the CAPTCHA was implemented improperly, but because the CAPTCHA itself is simply not effective against motivated attackers. The name CAPTCHA Defeat has therefore been adopted.

Denial of Inventory has been added since its defining characteristics do not match any of the 20 previously defined automated threat events. This threat is often seen in ecommerce applications where attackers add items to their basket to deny them to other users through the creation of a stock-out condition, and never actually check out. Similar allocation without purchase, or payment, or transaction completion, also occur in some non-ecommerce applications.

In addition to these changes, we have acknowledged additional contributors and reviewers, updated the countermeasures copy, added other names and examples to several threat events, and made numerous corrections to grammar, spelling mistakes, and typographical errors.

Colin Watson and Tin Zaw, 15th February 2018

Preface to v1.1

With the welcome addition of a co-project leader, and feedback from the community, we have been able to add significant new content to the *OWASP Automated Threat Handbook*.

A new addition for v1.1 is the work we have undertaken on enumeration and documentation of 14 automated threat countermeasure classes in the main body of the text of this document, and details of threat-specific explanations on each of the threat descriptions in the yellow threat event reference. The technology and vendor agnostic countermeasure classes attempt to group together the types of design, development and operational controls identified from research that are being used to partially or fully mitigate the likelihood and/or impact of automated threats to web applications.

Additionally more examples of symptoms for each threat have been provided, and we have tried to make them more consistent. The indicative diagrams and page keys have been recreated to improve legibility.

The automated web application threat events listed, their identity numbers and their names, are unchanged from the previous version (v1.0).

Colin Watson and Tin Zaw, 3rd November 2016

Preface to v1.0

Most web applications are not under a constant state of compromise, regardless of whether weaknesses and vulnerabilities are present. However, attackers are still using the software in a manner that causes significant pain to the owners/operators, and sometimes also the users.

Previous work on OWASP AppSensor (application-specific attack detection and response) has identified 50 or so types of detection points, and I had speculated about which detection points would be most beneficial to implement first. All AppSensor detection points should have an extremely low false positive attack detection rate so that normal usage is never flagged as malicious, but I wondered which detection points might identify attackers sooner than others - before some potential vulnerability could be targeted. What I needed was a list of threats (probably automated threats) that were not just attempting to exploit individual implementation bugs or misconfigurations. In other words, what are attackers actually doing most of the time?

And here I came across a blocker - there did not seem to be a clear categorisation or quantification of the actual automated threats most web application owners have to deal with day to day. These are also mostly not included in "breach" statistics and discussions, even though breaches of security are occurring. Instead, there is a greater focus on individual types of weaknesses and vulnerabilities, root cause analysis of data confidentiality breaches, and capabilities from vendors about product/services.

Some business owners are submerged in technical details that lead to a lack of comprehension about the relationships between security requirements, security activities during development, deployment and operation, and the operational impact of attacks. It also seems to be the case there is too great a focus on individual weaknesses/vulnerabilities in technical assurance activities, especially where the severity rating of each issue in isolation fails to provide the overall picture. For example, it is common for a number of individual low or medium severity issues to contribute to a much more significant business impact.

The potential misuse of valid functionality is also a concern, as this is an aspect where early design decisions have a significant effect on operational risk.

In order to quantify these threats, it is necessary to be able to name them. This did not seem to exist in the usual dictionaries and classifications. Therefore, I decided to produce an ontology of automated threats from the perspective of defenders. To contain the scope somewhat, I decided to focus solely on web applications, reducing the size of the task.

The first project output, this **OWASP Automated Threat Handbook**, includes the ontology. And now I am moving on to produce other materials for those bulding and defending web applications against automated threat events.

Colin Watson, 30th July 2015

Terminology

This handbook uses terminology based on the following sources:

1. Risk Taxonomy, Technical Standard, The Open Group, 2009
   http://pubs.opengroup.org/onlinepubs/9699919899/toc.pdf
2. NISTIR 7298 rev 2, NIST
   http://nvlpubs.nist.gov/nistpubs/ir/2013/NIST.IR.7298r2.pdf
3. OSI model, Wikipedia
   http://en.wikipedia.org/wiki/OSI_model
4. TCP/IP model, Wikipedia
   http://en.wikipedia.org/wiki/Internet_protocol_suite
5. Architecture of the World Wide Web, Volume One, W3C
   http://www.w3.org/TR/webarch/
6. Help and FAQ, W3C
   http://www.w3.org/Help/

Action
   An act taken against an asset by a threat agent. Requires first that contact occurs between the asset and threat agent (Ref 1).

Application
   Software that performs a business process, i.e. not system software. A software program hosted by an information system (Ref 2).

Application layer
   "Layer 7" in the OSI model (Ref 3) and "application layer" in the TCP/IP model (Ref 4).

Threat
   Anything that is capable of acting in a manner resulting in harm to an asset and/or organization; for example, acts of God (weather, geological events, etc.); malicious actors; errors; failures (Ref 1).

Threat Agent
   Any agent (e.g., object, substance, human, etc.) that is capable of acting against an asset in a manner that can result in harm (Ref 1).

Threat Event
   Occurs when a threat agent acts against an asset (Ref 1).

Web
   The World Wide Web (WWW, or simply Web) is an information space in which the items of interest, referred to as resources, are identified by global identifiers called Uniform Resource Identifiers (URI) (Ref 5). The first three specifications for Web technologies defined URLs, HTTP, and HTML (Ref 6).

Web application
   An application delivered over the web.

Introduction

Background

There is a significant body of knowledge about application vulnerability types, and some general consensus about identification and naming. But issues relating to the misuse of valid functionality (which may be caused by design flaws rather than implementation bugs) are less well defined. Yet these problems are seen day-in, day-out by web application owners. Some examples commonly referred to are:

- Account enumeration
- Aggregation
- Click fraud
- Comment spam
- Content scraping
- etc.

Excessive abuse of functionality is commonly misreported as application denial-of-service (DoS) attacks, such as HTTP flooding or application resource exhaustion, when in fact the DoS is a side-effect. Most of these problems seen regularly by web application owners are not listed in any OWASP Top Ten or in any other top issue list or dictionary.

This has contributed to inadequate visibility, and an inconsistency in naming such threats, with a consequent lack of clarity in attempts to address the issues.

Requirements

The aim was to produce an ontology that would provide a common language for developers, architects, operators, business owners, security engineers, purchasers, and suppliers/vendors, in order to facilitate clear communication and help tackle these issues. The project also intends to identify symptoms, mitigations and controls in this problem area. Like all OWASP outputs, everything is free and published using an open source licence.

Objectives

The objectives defined in early 2015 were:

- Provide a definition of the term "automated threat"
- Create a common vocabulary of automated threats and their relationships to each other that maintains consistency with existing literature.

This would involve creating a listing of vendor-neutral, technology-agnostic terms that describe real-world automated threats to web applications, at a level of abstraction suitable for application owners. The ontology and other supporting materials need to be practical and useful for a range of activities throughout a secure software development lifecycle (S-SDLC).

Scope

The focus for the project is the abuse of functionality - misuse of inherent functionality and related design flaws, some of which are also referred to as business logic flaws. There is no coverage of implementation bugs. It is neither the case that implementation bugs are not the target of attacks, nor that their exploitation cannot be automated, but there is much more knowledge published in that area with a greater agreement on terminology. The intention was that all the threats must require the web to exist for the threat to be materialised; thus attacks that can be achieved without the web are out of scope.

The threat events are scenarios which are seen commonly by real operating web applications, and are multi-step and/or highly iterative and/or multiple weaknesses involved, and not primarily about events that relate to the tool-based exploitation of single-issue vulnerabilities of individual web applications. Essentially the ontology is a list of concise answers to the operational question "what is happening right now?".

The summary definition created to describe this is "Threat events to web applications undertaken using automated actions".

The terms threat, threat event, web, applications and automated are defined in the terminology on page 2.

Some examples that are out of scope for this ontology are:

- Native mobile apps (but web application endpoint threats are in scope)
- Threats pre deployment (e.g. design, development, testing, deployment)
- Threats that affect web application businesses, but that are not undertaken using the web (e.g. in e-commerce: return fraud, wear & return fraud, not delivered fraud, price arbitrage, nearby address fraud, cross-merchant no-receipt returns, friendly fraud)
- Other layer 7 protocols including e.g. FTP, SMTP
- Host addressing and identification
- Attacks targeting network infrastructure
- Network, HTTP and SSL/TLS denial of service
- Physical and environmental attacks against components supporting web applications.

Therefore, attacks like phishing, pharming, and trojan distribution are excluded.

Research

Literature review

Work began on the project in late January 2015. Over 150 sources of information were identified, read and relevant threat information extracted. The full list of academic papers, blog posts, briefings, conference presentations, dictionaries, news stories, reports, technical papers and white papers is too long to include in this handbook but is published on the OWASP wiki:

https://www.owasp.org/index.php/OWASP_Automated_Threats_to_Web_Applications#tab=Bibliography

This created over 600 data points describing a mixture of threats, attacks and some vulnerabilities. Updates were periodically posted to the project pages on the OWASP wiki.

Analysis

In order to distil the data points to a more manageable scope, the information was first converted into a large-scale diagram. This attempted to remove duplication and highlight interrelationships. The diagram can be found on the OWASP wiki:

https://www.owasp.org/index.php/File:Automated-threats.pdf

Anything relating to exploitation of implementation bugs was excluded. Forty or so clusters of threats were extracted from this diagram, and this was reduced further to a slightly smaller number of candid threat event names. Work then began to identify inter-relationships, similarities, overlaps and unique aspects. This process was undertaken over 1-2 months and reduced the number of recommended threat event names to twenty-four. Further de-duplication reduced the final count to twenty. See below for a discussion of some of the candidate names that did not make the list. In v1.2 **OAT-021 Denial of Inventory** was added.

Peer review and comparison with other dictionaries, taxonomies and lists

The project was announced in the OWASP Foundation's Connector newsletter sent to 60,000+ recipients in April 2015. It was also highlighted in a two-side colour flyer included in every delegate's bag at AppSec EU 2015 in Amsterdam. A limited amount of peer review has been undertaken over a couple of months with:

- Professional colleagues
- Web application owners
- Web application developers
- Delegates at AppSec EU 2015 via an online and printed survey form
- One-to-one interviews with participants of the OWASP Project Summit 2015 in Amsterdam
- Others who found the project by search, or from coverage relating to a presentation given at AppSec USA in San Francisco in September 2015.

The peer review led to clearer scope, suggestions for additional threats, and changes to both the names and descriptions of the threat events. Further peer review would be welcome.

Three OWASP projects were reviewed at an early stage:

- The OWASP Top 10 [Web Application] Risks is the most well known OWASP output, but is a high-level awareness document with the aim to educate developers, designers, architects, managers, and organisations about the consequences of the most important web application security weaknesses; it highlights common and higher impact risks caused by both design flaws and implementation bugs; abuse of functionality is not a current top 10 item; no names from the OWASP Top 10 are included in the ontology
- The OWASP Top Ten [Web Application] Proactive Controls is a list of security techniques that should be included in every software development project; it is focused on reducing the incidence of weaknesses and vulnerabilities, but does not particularly address automated threats
- The OWASP WASC (Web Application Security Consortium) Web Hacking Incidents Database Project (WHID) classifies publicly known incidents using attack methods, weaknesses and outcomes. As such, it excludes incidents that were not reported, and thus is lacking in data relating to misuse of functionality. Some of the application denial of service incidents may include data that relates to other threat events described in the ontology.

The OWASP wiki includes many categorisations, one of which is "attack". The named items point to some automated threats, and were reviewed in the research stage. During the literature review and subsequent analysis and finalisation of the ontology, two reference sources were referred to again and again:

- Common Attack Pattern Enumeration and Classification (CAPEC) is a dictionary and classification taxonomy of known attacks on software. Its primary classification structures are Domains of attack (3000) and Mechanism of Attack (1000). While CAPEC includes many closely related threat events, and many detailed description of attacks, the dictionary does not provide coverage of all the automated threats identified in this ontology; the best match is often the category CAPEC-210 Abuse of Functionality; see Appendix B for a mapping of CAPEC category and attack pattern IDs to the ontology
- The Web Application Security Consortium (WASC) Threat Classification classifies weaknesses and attacks that can lead to the compromise of a website, its data, or its users; this was a useful source of automated threat information, but apart from authentication threats, most of the relevant concerns fall within a single classification (WASC-42 Abuse of Functionality).

But none of the above, nor Mitre's Common Weakness Enumeration (CWE) which is the most comprehensive dictionary of software weaknesses, provide the coverage and owner-viewpoint that this project aims to create.

The Ontology

Introduction

The original research, analysis and discussions with peers, completed over five months, whittled down the threat actions to a smaller core list of twenty in v1.0 (now twenty-one in v1.2), as described above.

The names used, combined with their defining characteristics, are taken from existing usage whenever possible. However, terminology is not used consistently within the literature sources reviewed, and also in some cases it was necessary to use a more generic term that captures the wider idea, instead of an individual common name. Furthermore, the intended outcomes of the threat action are usually unknown at the time of the action taking place, and thus outcome-related names were generally rejected. For example, is the creation of a fake account intended for distributing malware in user-generated content, or to manipulate search engine scoring, or to influence other users, or to explore the authenticated parts of the application?

The ontology is a list of threat event scenarios (when a threat agent acts against an asset, partially ordered in time) by software. The threat events cause a divergence from accepted behavior producing one or more undesirable effects on a web application. The list excludes tool-based exploitation of single-issue vulnerabilities.

The list

Full details of the finalised ontology threat events are provided in the beige coloured pages at the end of this handbook. A summary is provided below. Figure 1 lists the threat events ordered by ascending name, and Figures 2–5 illustrate some subsets.

The details at the end of this handbook categorise the threat events by:

- Sectors Targeted - Sectors that are targeted more commonly than others for the specific threat event are highlighted in amber; this is currently just the author's opinion, but the project is seeking information to define this aspect more accurately
- Parties Affected - Whether individuals, groups of people, the application owner and other parties are most often affected adversely by the threat event; the threat event may affect other parties depending upon the application and its data; the parties affected, excluding subsequent further misuse
- Data Commonly Misused - The types of data are web application specific; however, some threat events are more likely to occur for certain data types.

Each threat event is also cross-referenced with:

- Mitre CAPEC - best full and/or partial match CAPEC category IDs and/or attack pattern IDs
- WASC Threat Classification - best match to threat IDs
- Mitre Common Weakness Enumeration - closely related base, class & variant weakness IDs
- Matching pages defining terms classified as attacks on the OWASP wiki.

Figure 1: Automated Threat Events, ordered by ascending name

Identity Code	Name	Defining characteristics
OAT-020	Account Aggregation	Use by an intermediary application that collects together multiple accounts and interacts on their behalf
OAT-019	Account Creation	Create multiple accounts for subsequent misuse
OAT-003	Ad Fraud	False clicks and fraudulent display of web-placed advertisements
OAT-009	CAPTCHA Defeat	Solve anti-automation tests
OAT-001	Carding	Multiple payment authorisation attempts used to verify the validity of bulk stolen payment card data
OAT-010	Card Cracking	Identify missing start/expiry dates and security codes for stolen payment card data by trying different values
OAT-012	Cashing Out	Buy goods or obtain cash utilising validated stolen payment card or other user account data
OAT-007	Credential Cracking	Identify valid login credentials by trying different values for usernames and/or passwords
OAT-008	Credential Stuffing	Mass log in attempts used to verify the validity of stolen username/password pairs
OAT-021	Denial of Inventory	Deplete goods or services stock without ever completing the purchase or committing to the transaction
OAT-015	Denial of Service	Target resources of the application and database servers, or individual user accounts, to achieve denial of service (DoS)
OAT-006	Expediting	Perform actions to hasten progress of usually slow, tedious or time-consuming actions
OAT-004	Fingerprinting	Elicit information about the supporting software and framework types and versions
OAT-018	Footprinting	Probe and explore application to identify its constituents and properties
OAT-005	Scalping	Obtain limited-availability and/or preferred goods/services by unfair methods
OAT-011	Scraping	Collect application content and/or other data for use elsewhere
OAT-016	Skewing	Repeated link clicks, page requests or form submissions intended to alter some metric
OAT-013	Sniping	Last minute bid or offer for goods or services
OAT-017	Spamming	Malicious or questionable information addition that appears in public or private content, databases or user messages
OAT-002	Token Cracking	Mass enumeration of coupon numbers, voucher codes, discount tokens, etc
OAT-014	Vulnerability Scanning	Crawl and fuzz application to identify weaknesses and possible vulnerabilities

The detailed definations at the end of this handbook provide multiple classifications. Some are highlighted here as subsets of the twenty-one threat events.

Figure 2: Subset of Automated Threat Events Related to Account Credentials

Identity Code	Name	Defining characteristics
OAT-020	Account Aggregation	Use by an intermediary application that collects together multiple accounts and interacts on their behalf
OAT-019	Account Creation	Create multiple accounts for subsequent misuse
OAT-007	Credential Cracking	Identify valid login credentials by trying different values for usernames and/or passwords
OAT-008	Credential Stuffing	Mass log in attempts used to verify the validity of stolen username/password pairs

Figure 3: Subset of Automated Threat Events Related to Payment Cardholder Data

Identity Code	Name	Defining characteristics
OAT-001	Carding	Multiple payment authorisation attempts used to verify the validity of bulk stolen payment card data
OAT-010	Card Cracking	Identify missing start/expiry dates and security codes for stolen payment card data by trying different values
OAT-012	Cashing Out	Buy goods or obtain cash utilising validated stolen payment card or other user account data

Figure 4: Subset of Automated Threat Events Related to Vulnerability Identification

Identity Code	Name	Defining characteristics
OAT-004	Fingerprinting	Elicit information about the supporting software and framework types and versions
OAT-018	Footprinting	Probe and explore application to identify its constituents and properties
OAT-014	Vulnerability Scanning	Crawl and fuzz application to identify weaknesses and possible vulnerabilities

Figure 5: Subset of Automated Threat Events Related to Availability of Inventory to Legitimate Users

Identity Code	Name	Defining characteristics
OAT-021	Denial of Inventory	Deplete goods or services stock without ever completing the purchase or committing to the transaction
OAT-005	Scalping	Obtain limited-availability and/or preferred goods/services by unfair methods
OAT-011	Sniping	Collect application content and/or other data for use elsewhere

Mappings to other lists

The cross-references with the WASC Threat Classification and Mitre CAPEC, defined in the reference section at the back of this handbook, were examined further to determine how those differ from this ontology.

Figure 6: WASC Threat Classification view of the Automated Threat Events

The majority of the threat events are both the weakness WASC-21 Insufficient Anti-automation and the attack WASC-42 Abuse of Functionality. Three also relate to the attack WASC-11 Brute Force. WASC-45 Fingerprinting includes both **OAT-004 Fingerprinting** and **OAT-018 Footprinting**. Both WASC and this ontology have a unqiue category for Denial of Service.

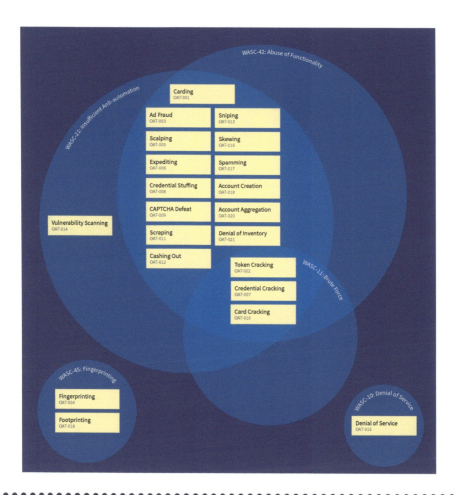

Figure 7: Mitre CAPEC view of the Automated Threat Events

Again, there are many threat events in the CAPEC-210 Abuse of Functionality. CAPEC also has additional categorisations for brute force attacks and denial of service. Two threat events, **OAT-009 CAPTCHA Defeat** and **OAT-014 Vulnerability Scanning**, do not appear to exist within CAPEC.

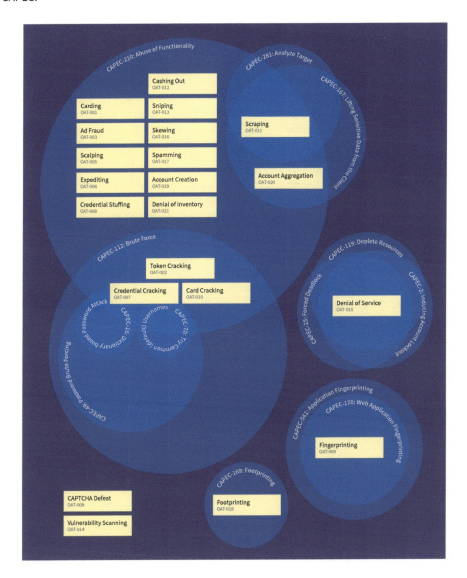

Notes

Threat event names

In all cases, "automated web application" could be used as a prefix to each name. Thus, for example, **OAT-012 Cashing Out** is concerned only with using web applications to obtain cash or goods; the ontology's scope excludes cashing out using ATMs. **OAT-015 Denial of Service** is web application denial of service, and not an SSL/TLS or network DoS. When referencing the terms in other contexts, it may be useful to ensure that the web application scope is identified.

Whenever possible, an existing term already used in literature or industry usage was preferred, but in many cases, it was difficult to identify such a term; as such, in some cases a more generic version had to be used. A good example of this is **OAT-013 Sniping**, where auction sniping is the most commonly cited case; it was determined that the characteristics of sniping also occur in threat events against other types of applications, and the selected name was thus made more general.

A handful of threat event names in the ontology are very specific since they are reported to occur frequently (e.g. **OAT-001 Carding, OAT-019 Account Creation**). Others are larger buckets (e.g. **OAT-011 Scraping, OAT-017 Spamming, OAT-014 Vulnerability Scanning**) that cannot be broken down easily without sharding the threat events into a multitude of sector-specific and function-specific examples.

For a while during the development of the ontology, aggregation of user accounts was temporarily included within **OAT-011 Scraping**. However, during final review it was felt the aspects of customer opt in, the intermediarisation and resulting disengagement were sufficiently different from scraping to make it a separate term. Furthermore, it was a threat commonly seen in financial services. The threat event was added back in as **OAT-020 Account Aggregation**. Other threat events described below were removed or consumed in other terms.

The only name newly created is **OAT-006 Expediting**, as there appeared to be a large number of sector-specific threats involving increased multi-step velocity that could otherwise not be aggregated together under a single name.

In v1.2 of this handbook, a new threat event **OAT-021 Denial of Inventory** was added since this type of stock depletion attack was not covered in any other OAT. Furthermore, the previously named OAT-009 CAPTCHA Bypass was renamed to **OAT-009 CAPTCHA Defeat** due to community feedback that the name could be misinterpreted too easily as circumventing CAPTCHAs due to an implementation bug, even though the name CAPTCHA Bypass is being used widely.

Threat event identity codes

To enable internal cross-referencing and referencing from elsewhere, each threat event has been given an identification (ID) code. This is a three-digit number prefixed by a hyphen and an abbreviation for OWASP Automated Threat (OAT) e.g. OAT-015. The ID codes were randomly assigned in an attempt to stop the ontology being seen as an ordered list, and also to ensure that neighbouring items are not necessarily related. Other cross-referencing is provided. Currently codes 001 to 021 are used, and it is expected the total number should be many fewer than fifty, unless many sub-items are ever added. Three digits, rather than two, were allotted in case the first digit is used for some other aspect in future, e.g. perhaps mobile application automated threat events could be 1xx, and 2xx for embedded software, etc.

Timing, duration and frequency

The scope focuses on threat events that involve multi-step and/or highly iterative interactions with the application. But by their nature, the identified threat events vary significantly in scale, and their timing, duration and frequency can all vary considerably. This is an area that could be explored further in future work.

Magnitude of impact

Events related to automated threats can have impacts on more than just the application owner. Individuals, third parties and even society can be adversely affected. This ontology does not attempt to provide information on, or rank the threat events in terms of impact, since it will be organisation, data, threat actor and victim-perspective specific. An organisation may choose to use its own risk assessment processes to rank these threats for each operational entity, or each market, or even by individual application.

The perpetrators

During the early stages of the ontology's creation, it was believed it would be possible to suggest which threat actors might be most likely to initiate the threat event. These threat agents might be groups like competitors, journalists, petty criminals, organised crime, nation states, etc and of course users such as citizens, clients, customers and employees. However, on further inspection, the threat agents appear to be more closely related to the type of data, and thus sector, rather than the particular threat event. Consequently, it is believed threat agents should be re-considered in future sector-specific views of the ontology.

Furthermore, some threat events may be undertaken by, or with the knowledge or implicit support of, application owners. For example, search engine indexing is generally encouraged due to the benefit of increased user traffic (**OAT-011 Scraping**); automated monitoring of web applications may be commissioned (**OAT-011 Scraping**); excessive account creation might contribute to enhanced market reputation when promoting the size of its customer base (**OAT-019 Account Creation**); the application owner with hosted advertisements could receive additional income for false impressions (**OAT-003 Ad Fraud**).

Fraud, legality and cheating

In general, the ontology tries to avoid the use of judgmental words like fraud. But in one case, the industry accepted term for the threat event includes this word: **OAT-003 Ad Fraud**.

In legal terms, whether an action is fraudulent depends on legislation and regulation in the relevant jurisdiction(s). Some of the events in this ontology may be illegal actions, or may be prohibited in a commercial contract. This will also depend upon the types of data handled, regulation of the application and its owner, and application-specific mandates like terms of use.

Rather than being illegal, some threat events will be considered cheating by other normal users, including **OAT-006 Expediting**, **OAT-005 Scalping**, **OAT-016 Skewing** and **OAT-013 Sniping**. These will be sector, application and culturally specific views, but can undermine user trust and the reputation of the application and its owner.

Terms excluded

A small number of threat events were removed during analysis and review based on discussions with peers and website owners. The primary reason for removal was either being out of scope, or because the term could not be adequately distinguished from another. Other people may have alternative views on these, so the discarded temporary working names and justifications are provided below alphabetically.

Application Consumption was a temporary working name given the misuse of the application to perform calculations, or process data, or perform other actions against other applications, hosts, or in the physical world, i.e. unauthorised real-time consumption of a normal application as if it were an API. Unlike data harvesting, in which information is gathered once or periodically, in consumption, the thought was the application is used on-demand by another system to provide calculated output, send requests to another application, or possibly affect physical assets the application provides direct control over. For example the application might be used to generate images or other files based on user input. In the second case, the application checks user submitted data (e.g. hostname, email address) by undertaking a reverse lookup, pingback or a reputation service check, contributing to a denial of service attack against that other host. In these situations, there seemed to be a close similarity with data harvesting and thus it was eventually concluded to be another example of **OAT-011 Scraping**.

Application Worms, also called cross-site scripting worms, are a combination of two different implementation flaws – cross-site request forgery (CSRF) and cross-site scripting (XSS). Additionally, the automation is undertaken by the web application itself in conjunction with often normal usage by innocent users. Therefore, it was decided this did not fall within the defined scope.

Asset Stripping was considered to encompass the removal of application stored non-data assets using compromised accounts and sessions, including data theft, collecting micro deposits, and collecting refunds. However, this asset removal, extraction or copying from applications used as repositories is no different from other data harvesting at the time of extraction. The only difference is the assets have value in other non-application contexts and may include fiat money, credit, refunds, financial instruments, reputation, virtual assets (e.g. status, score, virtual currency, identity), awards and points, and possible physical assets the application provides control over. But this value is often very subjective. Since these are data, it was considered this threat event was actually part of **OAT-011 Scraping**. The objectives of the attacker and consequences are data and application specific. Additionally, the transfer of money was included within **OAT-012 Cashing Out**. Consequently, Asset Stripping was not included as a separate term.

Attack Platform was at first used to describe the misuse of an application to mount automated attacks against another application or other external information system component. This would include reflected DoS, anti-spam check DoS, amplification DoS, and numerous HTML5 attacks. For example, if the application checks user submitted data (e.g. hostname, email address) by undertaking a reverse lookup, pingback or a reputation service check, contributing to a denial of service attack against that host. Or if an HTML application is compromised to undertake attacks against local and other remote systems. The affected host is not the application itself; instead, the application performs the attack on some other system. Ultimately, like the somewhat related Code Modification below, this was dropped from the ontology.

Code Modification relates to when the application logic is changed by modification of the source code, or the executing code, or the configuration, or some combination of these. The kinds of attacks included are malicious software download, malicious software update, advert injection, code tampering, DOM modification, web browser tools, form tampering, malicious software implanting, backdoor addition, shared data manipulation, use of untrusted code, memory modification, AngularJS attack, configuration data modification, exposed reflection, reflection injection, autobinding, and Rich Internet Application (RIA) attacks. The issue is made more significant with the growing use of client-side code. But it was felt these threats were related to lack of integrity checks, particularly during development and distribution, rather than being typical automated threats, and therefore Code Modification is not included in this ontology.

Form Hijacking (e.g. email spam, form to Email spam, SMS spam, use as a spam relay, and unsolicited bulk email) was initially thought to be a core threat event and would have been an ideal candidate for the threat event ontology. But again, it was realised that this is an implementation flaw that leverages vulnerabilities produced when an web server fails to validate input, and thus it does not fit into this ontology.

Man in the Browser (MitB), in which the attacker controls the user's web browser, so that information being transferred can be observed, intercepted and manipulated, was another threat event that was thought at the start of the project would be in the final ontology. The most well-known use case is to undertake financial fraud, and is the result of compromise of the user's device by a banking trojan, such as URLzone, Torpig, and Zeus. However, MitB can also be used for advert injection, and some simpler variants have been labelled Boy in the Browser (BitB). MitB/BitB are believed to be out-of-scope, since the trojan distribution and the interception/ change of information, are both occurring outside the web application's boundaries.

Reverse Engineering is exercising an application or part of an application with the intent to gain insight into how it is constructed and operates. The purpose may be to understand the inner workings, and may be used to determine business logic such as pricing models, reproduce the application elsewhere, or to assist with vulnerability exploitation and data compromise. It was decided to be an intended outcome of a combination of other threat actions - typically,

OAT-011 Scraping and **OAT-018 Footprinting**, which include the testing and collection of evidence to determine the underlying logic, structures, algorithms, functions, methods, and secrets of the application. Thus, as an outcome it was decided that Reverse Engineering is not a valid part of the ontology.

Countermeasures

Overview

In November 2016, Version 1.1 of this handbook added information about countermeasures. Some automated threats may be mitigated completely through appropriate development and/or operational controls. However, many automated threat events cannot usually be prevented completely if the attacker is determined and wants to target a single application, but it may still be possible to reduce the risk to an acceptable level. In all applications, builder-defender collaboration is key in controlling and mitigating automated threats – the best protected applications do not rely solely upon standalone external operational protections, but also have integrated protection built into the design.

Similarly to other types of application security threat, it is important to build consideration of automated threats into multiple phases of a secure software development lifecycle (S-SDLC). This includes:

- Educating and providing guidance to architects, developers, and testers
- Assessing risks during requirements definition
- Building countermeasures into the application and its environment
- Implementing adequate monitoring
- Tracking time spent dealing with automated threats
- Creating appropriate incident response measures.

Countermeasures are controls that attempt to mitigate the identified automated threats in three ways:

- Prevent - Controls to reduce the susceptibility to automated threats
- Detect - Controls to identify whether a user is an automated process rather than a human, and/or to identify if an automated attack is occurring, or occurred in the past
- Recover - Controls to assist response to incidents caused by automated threats, including to mitigate the impact of the attack, and to to assist return of the application to its normal state.

As mentioned previously, some threat events in this ontology may be illegal actions. Apart from subsequent contract-specific comments, web application owners should make themselves familiar with local legislation and regulation that affects the operation and use of their applications. For example, consumer protection legislation could reduce the likelihood of some automated threat events.

It is important to remember that not all automated usage of web applications is necessarily unwanted or malicious (e.g. search engine indexing at a reasonable rate and frequency is often very desirable). Some automated usage may also be implemented and/or authorised by the application's owner itself (e.g. periodic report generation, internal indexing, uptime/change/malware monitoring, vulnerability scanning).

Each owner must decide what is permissible, and for what period, and at what rate. If countermeasures are being applied to an existing web application, be careful of assumptions about what normal real user behaviour is – automated traffic may form a significant proportion of current usage already.

Classification of countermeasures

In an attempt to structure the countermeasure suggestions in this handbook, they are grouped using the following classes.

Figure 8: Automated Threat Countermeasure Classes

Countermeasure class		SDLC stage		Countermeasure type		
Keyword	Description	Builder	Defender	Prevent	Detect	Recover
Value	Removing or limiting the value of assets accessed using the application can reduce the benefits of an automated attack. This includes reviewing whether the data and/or functionality is necessary, or whether it can be changed to reduce its value to an attacker.	Y		Y		
Requirements	Identify relevant automated threats in security risk assessment, and assess effects of alternative countermeasures on functionality usability and accessibility. Use this to then define additional application development and deployment requirements	Y	Y	Y	Y	Y
Testing	Create abuse and misuse test cases that simulate automated web attacks.	Y		Y		
Capacity	Build adequate capacity so that any permitted and possible unwanted automated usage do not affect normal usage/performance.	Y	Y	Y		Y
Obfuscation	Hinder automated attacks by dynamically changing URLs, field names and content, or limiting access to indexing data, or adding extra headers/fields dynamically, or converting data into images, or adding page and session-specific tokens. This countermeasure also includes minimising information leakage, randomisation of functionality such that the application cannot be fully determined in advance, cloaking and other changes to confuse or misinform automated systems from understanding or fully mapping the application and its functions.	Y	Y	Y		
Fingerprinting	Consider identifying and restricting automated usage by automation identification techniques. Utilise user agent string, and/or HTTP request format (e.g. header ordering), and/or HTTP header anomalies (e.g. HTTP protocol, header inconsistencies), and/or device fingerprint content to determine whether a user is likely to be a human or not.	Y	Y	Y	Y	

Countermeasures

Countermeasure class		SDLC stage		Countermeasure type		
Keyword	Description	Builder	Defender	Prevent	Detect	Recover
Reputation	Consider identifying and restricting automated usage by reputation methods. Utilise reputation analysis of user identity (e.g. web browser fingerprint, device fingerprint, username, session, IP address/range/geolocation), and/or user behaviour (e.g. previous site, entry point, time of day, rate of requests, rate of new session generation, paths through application), and/or types of resources accessed (e.g. static vs dynamic, invisible/hidden links, robots.txt file, paths excluded in robots.txt, honeytrap resources, cache-defined resources), and/or types of resources not accessed (e.g. JavaScript generated links), and/or types of resources repeatedly accessed. Like Fingerprinting, used to determine whether a user is likely to be a human or not. Includes use of fraud detection systems and third-party deny/block lists, reputation, and credit-checking services.	Y	Y	Y	Y	
Authentication	Implement access control lists, or require users to be authenticated, or to re-authenticate, or behavioural biometrics, or to require greater identity verification to perform some functions including email address validation, use of puzzles/CAPTCHAs, out-of-band verification, password complexity and aging requirements, strong authentication, two-factor authentication, additional identity check at delivery/collection time, preventing concurrent usage with same identity, avoiding single-factor password based authentication, preventing the use of single sign on (SSO), and not supporting virtual currencies.	Y	Y	Y		
Rate	Set upper and/or lower limits and/or trend thresholds, and limit number and/or rate of usage per user, per group of users, per IP address/range, per device ID/fingerprint etc. Also limitation of value per event/transaction. Also includes use of queuing systems, user-prioritization functionality, and randomisation of asset allocation.	Y	Y	Y	Y	
Monitoring	Monitor errors, anomalies, function usage/sequencing, and provide alerting and/or monitoring dashboard. Monitor (e.g. moderate) user-generated content by automated systems.	Y	Y		Y	
Instrumentation	Build in application-wide instrumentation to perform real-time attack detection and automated response such as defined in OWASP AppSensor. Responses to an identified automated attack could be instigated by the application directly, and/or using some other system component such as a gateway, network firewall or application firewall. Responses can include increased monitoring, locking users out, blocking, delaying, changing behaviour, altering capacity/capability, enhanced identity authentication, CAPTCHA, penalty box, etc.	Y	Y	Y	Y	Y
Contract	Require users not to undertake automated attacks against the application through terms & conditions, contracts, and guidance. Understand contractual restrictions imposed by other parties on the application (e.g. service level agreements, financial credit).		Y	Y		
Response	Define actions in an incident response plan for various automated attack scenarios. Consider automated responses once an attack is detected. Consider using actual incident data to feed back into other countermeasures (e.g. Requirements, Testing, Monitoring).		Y			Y
Sharing	Share information about automated attacks, such as IP addresses or known violator device fingerprints, with others in same sector, with trade organisations, and with national CERTs.		Y		Y	

Many countermeasures should be built in, but there are a range of anti-automation and anti-bot vendors providing detection and prevention products and services, typically in the countermeasure classes of Capacity, Obfuscation, Fingerprinting, Reputation, Rate and Monitoring. Some such services/appliances span multiple classes. There are also open source options in these areas.

The effort of defining, implementing, configuring, tuning and maintaining countermeasures should not be underestimated. Existing solutions may help with these issues, especially where countermeasures are to be deployed across a portfolio of web applications.

The web application owner must decide what action to take when a particular type and level of automated threat event occurs, and what user(s) or IP(s), etc will the action(s) apply to. Actions might include:

- Increase monitoring
- Adapt the targeted function or whole application (e.g. raise authentication requirements, reduce functionality, limit exposure, disable)
- Block access.

For each threat and possible countermeasures, consider how they could be applied to particular user groups, or progressively activated to minimise the effect on normal users. Where "restricting automated usage" is mentioned, it is up to each affected party to determine what is permissible, achievable, relevant and practical. The possible side effects of actively responding to automated threat events should not be ignored.

Countermeasure selection

The relevant countermeasures should be drawn from an analysis of those that are:

- Generic and apply to all automated threats
- Specific to each particular relevant threat
- Specific to the application, its data and users.

For each OWASP Automated Threat (OAT) defined later in this handbook, threat-specific countermeasures in the above classes are provided on the second page. The guidance in this document is not specific to any particular application, or technology, or indeed product or service, but instead is provided as suggestions that can be considered, reviewed, and assessed, and their impact and efficacy considered for the particular web application.

The suggested countermeasures can reduce the likelihood of attack, and/or reduce the impact of a successful attack. The effect will depend greatly upon the type of application, types of data and types of users. Some countermeasures may be completely or relatively invisible to normal users, and others may be more visible but still acceptable in the context.

Use Case Scenarios

Introduction

The following scenarios and organisation names are completely fictitious.

Scenario: Defining application development security requirements

Cinnaminta SpA intends to build and launch a new multi-lingual and multi-currency e-commerce website. The development will be outsourced and Cinnaminta has been working on the functional design document. Among many other requirements, the application security specification requires that the website must not include any vulnerabilities identified in PCI DSS v3.1 Requirement 6.5, nor any other vulnerabilities that could affect the protection of payment cardholder data. Cinnaminta specifies that the website's payment functions must not be susceptible to the threat events **OAT-001 Carding** or **OAT-010 Card** Cracking, as defined in the *OWASP Automated Threat Handbook*. In addition, the application must interact with the company's existing fraud detection system to counter **OAT-012 Cashing Out**. The requirements are specified in terms of these threat events, rather than particular product or service categories. Development houses responding to the call for bids use the ontology to focus their answers to these aspects appropriately.

Scenario: Sharing intelligence within a sector

Unlimited Innovations Inc develops and supports patient-facing software solutions to a range of healthcare providers, many of which participate in the National Health Service Cyber Intelligence Sharing Center (NHS-CISC). Unlimited Innovations already builds continuous monitoring capabilities into its software and decides to provide an optional enhancement so that customers could choose to share their misuse event data with each other, to benefit from the combined threat intelligence. Rather than sharing large quantities of low-level data, Unlimited Innovations aggregates information and broadcasts validated and categorised threat data amongst the participating organisations. Automation attacks are classified according to the threat events defined in the *OWASP Automated Threat Handbook* so that each receiving party understands the nature of the threat. Even organisations that do not want to take part in this information sharing can benefit, since their own categorised information is made available to internal business management in the form of an easy-to-comprehend monitoring dashboard. The information gathered can also be fed into their other business information management systems to help improve patient service.

Scenario: Exchanging threat data between CERTs

National Computer Emergency Response Teams (CERTs) recognise that sharing of local information can contribute to worldwide prevention of cyber attacks. Despite advances in cooperation between CERTs, anything to increase continuity and interoperability, such as standards for data exchange, is encouraged. CERT Zog is concerned about the sparsity of application-specific data it receives, and also the classification of that data. It has a particular concern about attacks and breaches that affect sectors defined in Zog's 2015 national cyber security strategy. CERT Zog and its neighbour CERT Tarset agree to tag threat events using the **OWASP Automated Threat Handbook**, in order to add greater context to existing solutions being used for threat data exchange between them. The programme also collects sector metadata, so that all organisations within these can benefit from the centralised intelligence.

Scenario: Enhancing application penetration test findings

Specialist application security penetration testing firm Cherak Industries Pte Ltd works primarily for financial services companies in the banking and insurance sectors, and is looking to expand its business throughout Asia. Cherak has some innovative pen test result reporting systems which integrate with client software fault and vulnerability tracking systems, and it actively looks for methods to provide additional value to its clients. Cherak has identified that pen test clients would benefit from help in understanding the effects of combinations of vulnerabilities, especially design flaws, and has decided to utilise the **OWASP Automated Threat Handbook** to define and explain the automation-related threats. The individual vulnerabilities were scored as normal using CVSSv2 and v3, the matching CWEs identified, and mitigations in place documented. In addition, Cherak uses the threat events defined in the **OWASP Automated Threat Handbook** to help create a new section in the executive summary that explains how combinations of the issues found could lead to automation threats and the possible technical and business impacts. For example, an assessment for one client had identified weaknesses in authentication so that there is a risk of **OAT-008 Credential Stuffing**. The defined identifier was provided to the client, so its technical staff could refer to additional information on the OWASP website.

Scenario: Specifying service acquisition needs

Falstone Paradise Inc is concerned about malicious use of their portfolio of hotel and resort websites. The majority of the websites use a shared application platform, but there are some unique applications and a large number of other micro-sites, some of which use generic content management systems such as Wordpress and Drupal. Falstone Paradise has identified that its IT operations team are spending too much time dealing with the effects of automated misuse, such as cleaning up data, resetting customer accounts and providing extra capacity during attacks. Furthermore, the unwanted automation is also causing some instabilities leading to negative feedback from customers. Therefore Falstone Paradise decides to go out to the security marketplace to identify, assess and select products or services that might help address these automation issues for all its websites. Their buying team works with their information technology colleagues to write the detailed requirements in an Invitation to Tender (ITT) document. This describes the types of attacks its web applications are receiving, their frequency of occurrence and their magnitudes. These are defined according to the **OWASP Automated Threat Handbook**, so that vendors do not misunderstand the requirements, and each vendor's offering can be assessed against the particular automation threat events of concern.

Scenario: Characterising vendor services

Better Best Ltd has developed an innovative technology to help gaming companies defend against a range of automated threats that can otherwise permit cheating and distortion of the game, leading to disruption for normal players. The solution can be deployed on premises, but is also available in the cloud as a service. But Better Best is finding difficulty explaining its solution in the market place, especially since it does not fit into any conventional product category. Better Best decide to use the terminology and threat events listed in the *OWASP Automated Threat Handbook* to define their product's capabilities. They hope this will provide some clarity about their offering, and also demonstrate how their product can be used to replace more than one other conventional security device. Additionally, Better Best writes a white paper describing how their product has been successfully used by one of their reference customers Hollybush Challenge Games to protect against **OAT-006 Expediting**, **OAT-005 Scalping**, **OAT-016 Skewing** and **OAT-013 Sniping**.

Project Details

OWASP project

The wiki page for OWASP Automated Threats to Web Applications Project is:

https://www.owasp.org/index.php/OWASP_Automated_Threats_to_Web_Applications

It is classed as an OWASP Incubator project. The project's mailing list is:

https://lists.owasp.org/mailman/listinfo/automated_threats_to_web_applications

The project leaders are Colin Watson and Tin Zaw. The project has been rigorously reviewed, and was promoted to Labs status by OWASP in September 2017.

All OWASP Projects are run and developed by volunteers and rely on personal donations and sponsorship to continue their development. OWASP does not endorse or recommend commercial products or services, allowing our community to remain vendor neutral with the collective wisdom of the best minds in software security worldwide. This project has received the sponsorship element of corporate OWASP membership fees from Verizon Digital Media Services in 2016 and 2017, and Distil Networks in 2017. These have already contributed to the v1.2 production design costs, and will also be utilised to help raise awareness of the threats.

Source materials and outputs

Electronic versions of this handbook are maintained at these locations:

- Screen-optimised PDF
  https://www.owasp.org/index.php/File:Automated-threat-handbook.pdf
- Source Adobe InDesign
  https://www.owasp.org/index.php/File:Owasp-automated-threat-handbook-source-files.zip

Other working materials and outputs are:

- Print on demand book, colour
  http://www.lulu.com/spotlight/owasp
- Project flyer, 2-page PDF
  https://www.owasp.org/index.php/File:Automation-project-briefing.pdf
- Survey sheet used at Appsec EU 2015, PDF
  https://www.owasp.org/index.php/File:Automation-questionnaire-1v0.pdf
- Summary threats and attacks extracted during the research phase, large-scale PDF
  https://www.owasp.org/index.php/File:Automated-threats.pdf
- Project presentation, AppSec USA 2015
  https://www.owasp.org/index.php/File:Colinwatson-a-new-ontology-of-unwanted-automation.pptx
- Project presentation, AppSec Cali 2017
  https://www.owasp.org/index.php/File:BadBots_OWASP_AppSec_CA_2017.pptx

Handbook Roadmap

Ongoing improvement

It is hoped that the production of the ontology and handbook will lead to further discussion and debate and encourage additional project participants. For example, additional content and feedback are sought for the suggested countermeasures, effectiveness of alternative controls and threat identification metrics. A key area where help is required is in gathering data on the prevalence of these threats, where some form of data collection initiative is required.

People can contribute by posting ideas, suggestions, and other inputs to the project's public mailing list (see Project Details on the previous page).

Enhancements

It is also intended to develop sector-specific guides that include:

- Highest risk threat events
- Attacker motivations.

Retail and financial service sectors appear to be good candidates to begin with.

It would also be useful to summarise the developer-relevant information into a new Automated Threat Cheat Sheet, and contribute that to the OWASP Cheat Sheet Series.

The author also hopes this *OWASP Automated Threat Handbook*, with its industry cross-referencing, may be of help in contributing to Mitre's Common Weakness Risk Analysis Framework (CWRAF) and Common Attack Pattern Enumeration and Classification (CAPEC). In the future, the terms might also be useful for helping to describe some application events in the Mitre/DHS Structured Threat Information eXpression (STIX).

Automated Threat Event Reference

The following pages define each automated threat event in detail. The second page of each describes possible symptoms and will be extended in future to include security controls.

Automated Threat Event Reference

Key

Each threat event defined in the ontology is laid out on identically laid out pages. The annotated example below gives additional information about the various components. Further information is provided in the previous pages of this document.

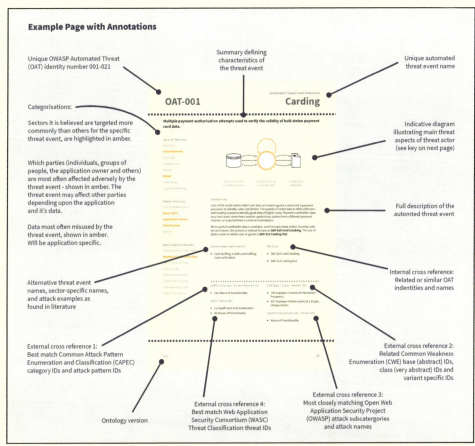

External cross-reference information sources:

1. Common Attack Pattern Enumeration and Classification (CAPEC), v2.6, The Mitre Corporation, July 2014
   https://capec.mitre.org
2. Common Weakness Enumeration (CWE), v2.8, The Mitre Corporation, July 2014
   http://cwe.mitre.org
3. Category: Attack, Open Web Application Security Project (OWASP)
   https://www.owasp.org/index.php/Category:Attack
4. The WASC Threat Classification, v2.0, Web Application Security Consortium, January 2010
   http://projects.webappsec.org/w/page/13246978/Threat%20Classification

OWASP Automated Threat Handbook Web Applications

Key

Each threat event includes an indicative diagram. The key below explains the meaning of the symbols used and an annotated example.

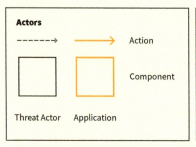

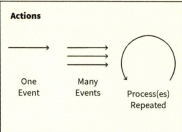

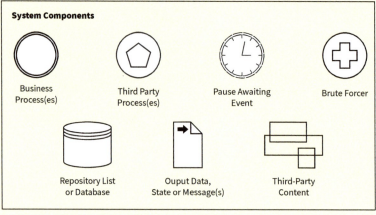

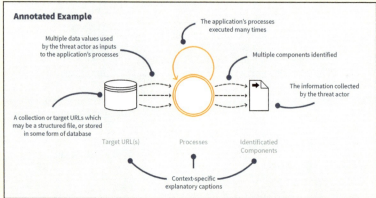

OAT-001

Carding

Multiple payment authorisation attempts used to verify the validity of bulk stolen payment card data.

Sectors Targeted

Education

Entertainment

Financial

Government

Health

Retail

Technology

Social Networking

Parties Affected

Few Individual Users

Many Users

Application Owner

Third Parties

Society

Data Commonly Misused

Authentication Credentials

Payment Cardholder Data

Other Financial Data

Medical Data

Other Personal Data

Intellectual Property

Other Business Data

Public Information

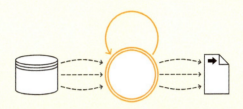

Stolen Payment Cardholder Data — Card Payment Process — Validated Cardholder Data

Description

Lists of full credit and/or debit card data are tested against a merchant's payment processes to identify valid card details. The quality of stolen data is often unknown, and Carding is used to identify good data of higher value. Payment cardholder data may have been stolen from another application, stolen from a different payment channel, or acquired from a criminal marketplace.

When partial cardholder data is available, and the expiry date and/or security code are not known, the process is instead known as **OAT-010 Card Cracking**. The use of stolen cards to obtain cash or goods is **OAT-012 Cashing Out**.

Other Names and Examples

- Card stuffing; Credit card stuffing; Card verification

See Also

- OAT-010 Card Cracking
- OAT-012 Cashing Out

CAPEC Category / Attack Pattern IDs

- 210 Abuse of Functionality

WASC Threat IDs

- 21 Insufficient Anti-Automation
- 42 Abuse of Functionality

CWE Base / Class / Variant IDs

- 799 Improper Control of Interaction Frequency
- 837 Improper Enforcement of a Single, Unique Action

OWASP Attack Category / Attack IDs

- Abuse of Functionality

v1.2

Carding

OAT-001

Multiple payment authorisation attempts used to verify the validity of bulk stolen payment card data.

Possible Symptoms

- Elevated basket abandonment
- Reduced average basket price
- Higher proportion of failed payment authorisations
- Disproportionate use of the payment step
- Increased chargebacks
- Multiple failed payment authorizations from the same user and/or IP address and/or User Agent and/or session and/or device ID/fingerprint

Suggested Threat-Specific Countermeasures

Class	Threat-Specific Comments
Value	Consider fully outsourcing all payment aspects to an appropriate payment services provider (PSP) that has its own countermeasures in place for OAT-001. Consider increasing the minimum checkout value. Consider removing payment by card completely if alternatives are available and suitable.
Requirements	Document acceptable use of payment functions; define additional requirements.
Testing	Define test cases for **OAT-001 Carding** that confirm the application will detect and/or prevent users attempting to use cardholder data in bulk.
Capacity	Not applicable
Obfuscation	Consider randomising the content and URLs of payment form and payment submission pages, tying these changes to the individual user's session, verifying the changes at each payment step, and restricting any identified automated usage.
Fingerprinting	Consider identifying and restricting automated usage by fingerprinting the User Agent for its unique characteristics.
Reputation	Consider identifying and restricting automated usage by reputation methods. In particular, consider using geolocation and/or IP address block lists to prevent access to payment parts of the application. Consider using address and card reputation services. Consider adding delays in the checkout steps for new and/or infrequent customers, and for smaller checkout baskets, and for users that appear to have skipped directly to payment bypassing basket addition and checkout, or are using known fraudulent payment cards.
Authentication	Consider removing guest checkout and/or requiring greater identity authentication for customers. Consider adding a CAPTCHA step for new and/or infrequent customers, and for smaller checkout baskets, and for users that appear to have skipped directly to payment. Consider implementing 3D Secure for some or all card payments. Consider pre-registering users and implementing strong authentication for access to any exposed payment APIs.
Rate	Limit the number of card authorisation attempts per session/user/IP address/device/fingerprint.
Monitoring	Log abandoned baskets; monitor rates. Log basket payment amount (and currency); monitor average value trends. Log successful and failed card authorisations; monitor rates relative to normal activity and also relative the usage of the rest of the application. Track chargeback amounts and trends.
Instrumentation	Consider blocking or delaying payment function access by users in a particular session, IP address/range or geolocation or everyone once Monitoring has identified a real Carding attack, or other anomalous behaviour that has identified the user as an attacker.
Contract	Use application access/use terms and conditions (T&Cs) to explicitly ban users from using the payment parts of the application to undertake Carding, and consider requiring opt-in agreement to these before the application can be used (or as part of the checkout process). Define service limits for any payment APIs.
Response	Define actions to be taken in the event a Carding attack is detected.
Sharing	Participate in e-commerce threat intelligence exchanges and contribute attack data to sector-wide sharing systems. Participate in any fraud detection and prevention arrangements offered by the payment service provider or merchant bank.

Automated Threat Event Reference

OAT-002
Token Cracking

Mass enumeration of coupon numbers, voucher codes, discount tokens, etc.

PARTIES AFFECTED

Education
Entertainment
Financial
Government
Health
Retail
Technology
Social Networking

PARTIES AFFECTED

Few Individual Users
Many Users
Application Owner
Third Parties
Society

DATA COMMONLY MISUSED

Authentication Credentials
Payment Cardholder Data
Other Financial Data
Medical Data
Other Personal Data
Intellectual Property
Other Business Data
Public Information

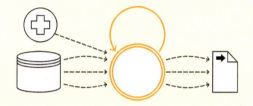

Token Dictionaries, Lists, Randoms & Brute Forcing — Token Code Validation Process(es) — Validated Token Codes

DESCRIPTION

Identification of valid token codes providing some form of user benefit within the application. The benefit may be a cash alternative, a non-cash credit, a discount, or an opportunity such as access to a limited offer.

For cracking of usernames, see **OAT-007 Credential Cracking** instead.

OTHER NAMES AND EXAMPLES

Coupon guessing; Voucher, gift card and discount enumeration

SEE ALSO

- OAT-007 Credential Cracking
- OAT-011 Scraping
- OAT-012 Cashing Out

CAPEC CATEGORY / ATTACK PATTERN IDS

- 112 Brute Force
- 210 Abuse of Functionality

WASC THREAT IDS

- 11 Brute Force
- 21 Insufficient Anti-Automation
- 42 Abuse of Functionality

CWEs

- 799 Improper Control of Interaction Frequency
- 837 Improper Enforcement of a Single, Unique Action

OWASP ATTACKS

- Abuse of Functionality
- Brute Force Attack

OWASP Automated Threat Handbook Web Applications

Token Cracking   OAT-002

Mass enumeration of coupon numbers, voucher codes, discount tokens, etc.

POSSIBLE SYMPTOMS

- Multiple failed token attempts from the same user and/or IP address and/or User Agent and/or device ID/fingerprint
- High number of failed token attempts

SUGGESTED THREAT-SPECIFIC COUNTERMEASURES

Class	Threat-Specific Comments
Value	Consider decreasing the attractiveness of tokens in the application, by removing them, reducing their value, or limiting their life or scope of use. Consider disallowing vouchers schemes.
Requirements	Document all locations where coupon numbers, voucher codes, discount tokens and similar elements are used in the application. Specify limits on acceptable use of each function related each token; define additional requirements.
Testing	Define test cases for **OAT-002 Token Cracking** that confirm the application will detect and/or prevent users trying to enumerate and/or use tokens at a disproportionate scale.
Capacity	Not applicable
Obfuscation	Consider randomising the content and URLs of token submission pages, tying these changes to the individual user's session, verifying the changes at each token-related request, and restricting any identified automated usage.
Fingerprinting	Consider identifying and restricting automated usage by fingerprinting the User Agent for its unique characteristics.
Reputation	Consider identifying and restricting automated usage by reputation methods.
Authentication	Consider requiring identity authentication, re-authentication or some other increased authentication assurance for access to areas where tokens are generated or consumed.
Rate	Limit the number of failed token submission attempts per session/user/IP address/device/fingerprint.
Monitoring	Log successful and failed token submissions; monitor rates relative to normal activity and also relative the usage of the rest of the application. Where applicable, track token creation trends.
Instrumentation	Consider blocking or delaying access by users in a particular session, IP address/range or geolocation once Monitoring has identified a real Token Cracking attack, or other anomalous behaviour that has identified the user as an attacker.
Contract	Define T&Cs to explicitly ban users from misusing the application to undertake Token Cracking, and similar activities. Define service limits for any token validation or creation APIs.
Response	Define actions to be taken in the event a Token Cracking attack is detected.
Sharing	Participate in relevant threat intelligence exchanges and contribute attack data to sector-wide sharing systems.

Automated Threat Event Reference

OAT-003

Ad Fraud

False clicks and fraudulent display of web-placed advertisements.

SECTORS TARGETED
Education
Entertainment
Financial
Government
Health
Retail
Technology
Social Networking

Target URL(s) and/or Advertisements → Third Party Advertisement Content → Process Clicks & Impressions → Elevated Count

PARTIES AFFECTED
Few Individual Users
Many Users
Application Owner
Third Parties
Society

DESCRIPTION

Falsification of the number of times an item such as an advert is clicked on, or the number of times an advertisement is displayed. Performed by owners of web sites displaying ads, competitors and vandals.

See **OAT-016** Skewing instead for similar activity that does not involve web-placed advertisements.

DATA COMMONLY MISUSED
Authentication Credentials
Payment Cardholder Data
Other Financial Data
Medical Data
Other Personal Data
Intellectual Property
Other Business Data
Public Information

OTHER NAMES AND EXAMPLES

Advert fraud; Adware traffic; Click bot; Click fraud; Hit fraud; Impression fraud; Pay per click advertising abuse; Phoney ad traffic

SEE ALSO

- OAT-016 Skewing

CAPEC CATEGORY / ATTACK PATTERN IDS

- 210 Abuse of Functionality

WASC THREAT IDS

- 21 Insufficient Anti-Automation
- 42 Abuse of Functionality

CWEs

-

OWASP ATTACKS

- Abuse of Functionality

…

Ad Fraud

OAT-003

False clicks and fraudulent display of web-placed advertisements.

…

POSSIBLE SYMPTOMS

- Common patterns — such as the same Referer or User Agent — in click or impression spikes (peaks)
- Low conversion ratios during the spikes
- Unusual peaks in the number of clicks or impressions
- No increase in the number of conversions during peaks in impressions or clicks
- Drop in the number of page views during peaks in impressions or clicks
- Higher bounce rate during peaks in impressions or clicks

SUGGESTED THREAT-SPECIFIC COUNTERMEASURES

Builder-defender collaboration is key in controlling and mitigating this threat.

Class	Threat-Specific Comments
Value	Consider limiting the maximum benefit offered in defined time periods. Consider using multi-touch attribution instead of last click. Consider not hosting advertisements in some parts of the application. Consider serving "house" or low-value ads to suspect requests.
Requirements	Document all types, locations, revenue methods, and any providers of advertising. Define logging requirements that capture sufficient information for thorough analysis of conversion and common patterns. Define downstream workflow systems to determine quality of clicks or impressions. Have downstream systems consume information produced by the company's own systems as well as information fed by outside vendors – such as IP reputation – in determining quality of clicks or impressions. Define additional requirements.
Testing	Define test cases for **OAT-003 Ad Fraud** that confirm a variety of advertising-related fraud techniques are detectable.
Capacity	Not applicable
Obfuscation	Not applicable
Fingerprinting	Consider identifying and restricting automated usage by fingerprinting the User Agent for its unique characteristics and using the information to reject or restrict value of related clicks/impressions.
Reputation	Subscribe to IP reputation data and use it as a factor in determining click or impression quality.
Authentication	Consider requiring identity authentication, re-authentication or some other increased authentication assurance in areas where advertisements are displayed so that clicks, impressions, etc can be more easily attributed.
Rate	Not applicable
Monitoring	Log impressions, clicks and conversions; monitor relative rates. Identify internal vs external users, and human vs system users where known. Perform analysis, near real-time if possible, for common patterns in users' system fingerprints, IP addresses and HTTP headers (such as User Agent, cookies, etc.), especially for requests during traffic peaks, and track relationship to conversation ratios.
Instrumentation	Not applicable
Contract	Build limitations in liability (of payment) on fraudulent clicks and impressions in contractual and commercial terms. Define end user T&Cs, employee contracts, corporate policies etc to ensure users understand that Ad Fraud is not permissible.
Response	Define actions to be taken in the event an Ad Fraud attack is detected.
Sharing	Participate in any fraud detection and prevention arrangements offered by the advertisement providers.

…

Automated Threat Event Reference

OAT-004

Fingerprinting

Elicit information about the supporting software and framework types and versions.

Sectors Targeted

Education

Entertainment

Financial

Government

Health

Retail

Technology

Social Networking

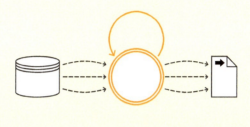

Target URL(s)   Processes   Identificatied Components

Parties Affected

Few Individual Users

Many Users

Application Owner

Third Parties

Society

Data Commonly Misused

Authentication Credentials

Payment Cardholder Data

Other Financial Data

Medical Data

Other Personal Data

Intellectual Property

Other Business Data

Public Information

Description

Specific requests are sent to the application eliciting information in order to profile the application. This probing typically examines HTTP header names and values, session identifier names and formats, contents of error page messages, URL path case sensitivity, URL path patterns, file extensions, and whether software-specific files and directories exist. Fingerprinting is often reliant on information leakage and this profiling may also reveal some network architecture/topology. The fingerprinting may be undertaken without any direct usage of the application, e.g. by querying a store of exposed application properties such as held in a search engine's index.

Fingerprinting seeks to identity application components, whereas **OAT-018 Footprinting** is a more detailed analysis of how the application works.

Other Names and Examples

Google dorking; Google hacking; Shodaning; Target acquisition; Target scanning; Finding potentially vulnerable applications; Reconnaissance; URL harvesting; Web application fingerprinting

See Also

- OAT-011 Scraping
- OAT-018 Footprinting

CAPEC Category / Attack Pattern IDs

- 541 Application Fingerprinting
- 170 Web Application Fingerprinting

WASC Threat IDs

- 45 Fingerprinting

CWEs

- 200 Information Exposure

OWASP Attacks

-

v1.2

Fingerprinting

OAT-004

Elicit information about the supporting software and framework types and versions.

POSSIBLE SYMPTOMS

- Single HTTP requests (just one single request and no more from that browser/session/device/fingerprint)
- Often none, but possibly requests for a wide range of missing resources
- Requests for resources that are rarely requested

SUGGESTED THREAT-SPECIFIC COUNTERMEASURES

Class	Threat-Specific Comments
Value	Remove or mask system information leakages (e.g. HTTP headers, error messages, URL paths, and file extensions).
Requirements	Not applicable
Testing	Utilise automated scanners to ensure no information on application components is being leaked.
Capacity	Not applicable
Obfuscation	Consider masking or changing or removing software and framework details from all types of responses (e.g .system details in HTTP headers can be removed if using an HTTP proxy or by configuring the web server). Consider preventing indexing by search engines.
Fingerprinting	Not applicable
Reputation	Consider restricting access from IP addresses with low reputation.
Authentication	Consider requiring normal or strong authentication for some or all parts of the application.
Rate	Not applicable
Monitoring	Not applicable
Instrumentation	Not applicable
Contract	Not applicable
Response	Not applicable
Sharing	Not applicable

Automated Threat Event Reference

OAT-005

Scalping

Obtain limited-availability and/or preferred goods/services by unfair methods.

Sectors Targeted

Education

Entertainment

Financial

Government

Health

Retail

Technology

Social Networking

Parties Affected

Few Individual Users

Many Users

Application Owner

Third Parties

Society

Data Commonly Misused

Authentication Credentials

Payment Cardholder Data

Other Financial Data

Medical Data

Other Personal Data

Intellectual Property

Other Business Data

Public Information

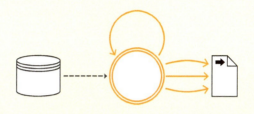

Target Assest Opportunity → Booking or Purchase Process(es) → Acquired Asset Identities

Description

Acquisition of goods or services using the application in a manner that a normal user would be unable to undertake manually.

Although Scalping may include monitoring awaiting availability of the goods or services, and then rapid action to beat normal users to obtain these, Scalping is not a "last minute" action like **OAT-013 Sniping**, nor just related to automation on behalf of the user such as in **OAT-006 Expediting**. This is because Scalping includes the additional concept of limited availability of sought-after goods or services, and is most well known in the ticketing business where the tickets acquired are then resold later at a profit by the scalpers/touts. This can also lead to a type of user denial of service, since the goods or services become unavailable rapidly.

Other Names and Examples

Bulk purchase; Purchase automaton; Purchase bot; Restaurant table/hotel room reservation speed-booking; Queue jumping; Sale stampede; Secondary ticketing; Ticket resale; Ticket scalping; Ticket touting

See Also

- OAT-006 Expediting
- OAT-013 Sniping
- OAT-015 Denial of Service
- OAT-021 Denial of Inventory

CAPEC Category / Attack Pattern IDs

- 210 Abuse of Functionality

WASC Threat IDs

- 21 Insufficient Anti-Automation
- 42 Abuse of Functionality

CWEs

- 799 Improper Control of Interaction Frequency
- 837 Improper Enforcement of a Single, Unique Action

OWASP Attacks

- Abuse of Functionality

v1.2

Scalping OAT-005

Obtain limited-availability and/or preferred goods/services by unfair methods.

Possible Symptoms

- High peaks of traffic for certain limited-availability goods or services
- Increased circulation of limited goods reselling on secondary market

Suggested Threat-Specific Countermeasures

Class	Threat-Specific Comments
Value	Consider increasing the real or apparent availability of the goods/services. Consider limiting the value of the good/service by tying its subsequent use specifically to one user, thus reducing its resale value. Consider penalising rapid and/or repeated purchase.
Requirements	Document acceptable use of relevant functions (e.g. selection, ordering, booking, reserving, checkout); define additional requirements.
Testing	Define test cases for OAT-005 Scalping that confirm the application will detect and/or prevent users attempting to obtain limited-availability/preferred goods by unfair methods.
Capacity	Not applicable
Obfuscation	Consider randomising the content and URLs of relevant functions, tying these changes to the individual user's session, verifying the changes at each request, and restricting any identified automated usage.
Fingerprinting	Consider identifying and restricting automated usage by fingerprinting the User Agent for its unique characteristics.
Reputation	Consider identifying and restricting automated usage by reputation methods. In particular, consider using geolocation and/or IP address block lists and/or reputation services to prevent access to the good/service allocation functions.
Authentication	Consider requiring identity authentication, re-authentication or some other increased authentication assurance for access to relevant functions, for all users or when there is a suspicion that Scalping is occurring.
Rate	Consider adding random delays in responses. Consider implementing queuing systems.
Monitoring	Log good/service allocation; monitor rate of depletion. Monitor availability of goods on secondary markets.
Instrumentation	Consider blocking or delaying access or delaying access by users in a particular session, IP address/range or geolocation once Monitoring has identified a real Scalping attack, or other anomalous behaviour that has identified the user as an attacker.
Contract	Define T&Cs to explicitly define acceptable use of the application and permissible re-sale/re-use of the good/service by another party. Use employment contracts to ban staff from leaking information about availability and other properties of upcoming goods/service releases.
Response	Define actions to be taken in the event a Scalping attack is detected.
Sharing	Participate in threat intelligence exchanges and contribute Scalping attack data to sector-wide sharing systems.

Automated Threat Event Reference

OAT-006
Expediting

Perform actions to hasten progress of usually slow, tedious or time-consuming actions.

SECTORS TARGETED

Education
Entertainment
Financial
Government
Health
Retail
Technology
Social Networking

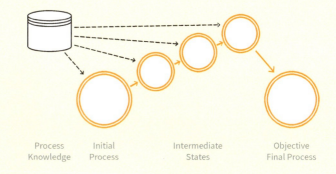

Process Knowledge | Initial Process | Intermediate States | Objective Final Process

PARTIES AFFECTED

Few Individual Users
Many Users
Application Owner
Third Parties
Society

DATA COMMONLY MISUSED

Authentication Credentials
Payment Cardholder Data
Other Financial Data
Medical Data
Other Personal Data
Intellectual Property
Other Business Data
Public Information

DESCRIPTION

Using speed to violate explicit or implicit assumptions about the application's normal use to achieve unfair individual gain, often associated with deceit and loss to some other party.

In contrast to **OAT-016 Skewing** which affects metrics, Expediting is purely related to faster progression through a series of application processes. And **OAT-017 Spamming** is different to Expediting, since the focus of spam is to add information, and may not involve the concept of process progression.

OTHER NAMES AND EXAMPLES

Algorithmic trading; Automated stock trading; Betting automation; Game automation; Gaming bot; Gold farming; Financial instrument dealing; High frequency trading; Last look trade; Mining; Purchase automation; Ticketing automation; Trading automation; Virtual wealth generation bot

SEE ALSO

- OAT-005 Scalping
- OAT-013 Sniping
- OAT-016 Skewing
- OAT-017 Spamming

CAPEC CATEGORY / ATTACK PATTERN IDs

- 210 Abuse of Functionality

WASC THREAT IDs

- 21 Insufficient Anti-Automation
- 42 Abuse of Functionality

CWEs

- 841 Improper Enforcement of Behavioral Workflow

OWASP ATTACKS

- Abuse of Functionality

v1.2

OWASP Automated Threat Handbook Web Applications

Expediting

OAT-006

Perform actions to hasten progress of usually slow, tedious or time-consuming actions.

POSSIBLE SYMPTOMS

- Uncharacteristically fast progress through multi-stage processes

SUGGESTED THREAT-SPECIFIC COUNTERMEASURES

Class	Threat-Specific Comments
Value	Consider adding penalties for hastened progress.
Requirements	Document acceptable use of each process exposed by the application; define additional requirements.
Testing	Define test cases for **OAT-006 Expediting** that confirm the application will detect and/or prevent users attempting to violate explicit or implicit assumptions about normal use.
Capacity	Not applicable
Obfuscation	Randomise the content and URLs, tying these changes to the individual user's session, verifying the changes at each request, and restricting any identified automated usage.
Fingerprinting	Consider identifying and restricting automated usage by fingerprinting the User Agent for its unique characteristics.
Reputation	Consider identifying and restricting automated usage by reputation methods.
Authentication	Consider requiring identity authentication, re-authentication or some other increased authentication assurance for access to relevant processes for all users or when there is a suspicion that Expediting is occurring.
Rate	Consider adding random delays in responses.
Monitoring	Log process step completion timestamps and rate of data entry; monitor for faster-than-average progress.
Instrumentation	Consider blocking or delaying access or delaying access by users in a particular session, IP address/range or geolocation once Monitoring has identified a real Expediting attack, or other anomalous behaviour that has identified the user as an attacker.
Contract	Define T&Cs to explicitly define acceptable use.
Response	Define actions to be taken in the event an Expediting attack is detected.
Sharing	Not applicable

OAT-007

Automated Threat Event Reference

Credential Cracking

Identify valid login credentials by trying different values for usernames and/or passwords.

Sectors Targeted

Education
Entertainment
Financial
Government
Health
Retail
Technology
Social Networking

Credential Dictionaries, Randoms & Brute Forcing — User Identity Authentication Process — Validated Credentials

Parties Affected

Few Individual Users
Many Users
Application Owner
Third Parties
Society

Description

Brute force, dictionary (word list) and guessing attacks used against authentication processes of the application to identify valid account credentials. This may utilise common usernames or passwords, or involve initial username evaluation.

The use of stolen credential sets (paired username and passwords) to authenticate at one or more services is **OAT-008 Credential Stuffing**.

Data Commonly Misused

Authentication Credentials
Payment Cardholder Data
Other Financial Data
Medical Data
Other Personal Data
Intellectual Property
Other Business Data
Public Information

Other Names and Examples

Brute-force attacks against sign-in; Brute forcing log-in credentials; Brute-force password cracking; Cracking login credentials; Password brute-forcing; Password cracking; Reverse brute force attack; Username cracking; Username enumeration

See Also

- OAT-002 Token Cracking
- OAT-008 Credential Stuffing
- OAT-019 Account Creation

CAPEC Category / Attack Pattern IDs

- 16 Dictionary-based Password Attack
- 49 Password Brute Forcing
- 70 Try Common(default) Usernames and Passwords
- 112 Brute Force

WASC Threat IDs

- 11 Brute Force
- 21 Insufficient Anti-Automation
- 42 Abuse of Functionality

CWEs

- 307 Improper Restriction of Excessive Authentication Attempts
- 799 Improper Control of Interaction Frequency
- 837 Improper Enforcement of a Single, Unique Action

OWASP Attacks

- Abuse of Functionality
- Brute Force Attack

v1.2

OWASP Automated Threat Handbook Web Applications

Credential Cracking OAT-007

Identify valid login credentials by trying different values for usernames and/or passwords.

Possible Symptoms

- Relatively high number of failed login attempts
- Many requests containing variations on account name and/or password
- Elevated account lock rate
- Increased customer complaints of account hijacking through help center or social media outlets

Suggested Threat-Specific Countermeasures

Class	Threat-Specific Comments
Value	Not applicable
Requirements	Document acceptable use of authentication functions; define additional requirements.
Testing	Define test cases for **OAT-007 Credential Cracking** that confirm the application will detect and/or prevent users attempting to guess usernames and/or passwords.
Capacity	Not applicable
Obfuscation	Consider randomising the content and URLs of authentication form pages, tying these changes to the individual user's session, verifying the changes at each authentication step, and restricting any identified automated usage.
Fingerprinting	Consider identifying and restricting automated usage by fingerprinting the User Agent for its unique characteristics.
Reputation	Consider identifying and restricting automated usage by reputation methods. In particular, consider using geolocation and/or IP address block lists to prevent access to authentication functions.
Authentication	Consider preventing users from selecting either common or weak passwords. Consider performing incremental account lock out to accounts with suspected login attempts. Consider enhancing authentication by adding CAPTCHA, or adding application-specific challenge questions, or using strong authentication such as two factor authentication. Consider stricter measures for user accounts with greater permissions (e.g. staff, moderators, content administrators, system accounts). Consider pre-registering users and implementing strong authentication for access to any exposed authentication APIs.
Rate	Limit the number of authentication attempts (success and failure) per session/user/IP address/device/fingerprint.
Monitoring	Log successful and unsuccessful authentication attempts per username/IP/session across all functions (register, logon, password reset, password change, username change, re-authentication, etc) and channels (web, mobile app, call centre, etc); monitor rates. Monitor geolocation relative to previous logins for each user. Identify account hijacking reports from customers; monitor trends.
Instrumentation	Consider blocking or delaying access by users in a particular session, IP address/range or geolocation or everyone once Monitoring has identified a real Credential Cracking attack, or other anomalous behaviour that has identified the user as an attacker.
Contract	Define service limits for any authentication APIs.
Response	Define actions to be taken in the event a Credential Cracking attack is detected.
Sharing	Participate in threat intelligence exchanges and contribute attack data to sector-wide sharing systems.

Automated Threat Event Reference

OAT-008

Credential Stuffing

Mass log in attempts used to verify the validity of stolen username/password pairs.

SECTORS TARGETED

Education

Entertainment

Financial

Government

Health

Retail

Technology

Social Networking

PARTIES AFFECTED

Few Individual Users

Many Users

Application Owner

Third Parties

Society

DATA COMMONLY MISUSED

Authentication Credentials

Payment Cardholder Data

Other Financial Data

Medical Data

Other Personal Data

Intellectual Property

Other Business Data

Public Information

Stolen Log In Credentials → User Identity Authentication Process → Validated Credentials

DESCRIPTION

Lists of authentication credentials stolen from elsewhere are tested against the application's authentication mechanisms to identify whether users have re-used the same login credentials. The stolen usernames (often email addresses) and password pairs could have been sourced directly from another application by the attacker, purchased in a criminal marketplace, or obtained from publicly available breach data dumps.

Unlike **OAT-007 Credential Cracking,** Credential Stuffing does not involve any brute-forcing or guessing of values; instead credentials used in other applications are being tested for validity.

OTHER NAMES AND EXAMPLES

Account checker attack; Account checking; Account takeover; Account takeover attack; Login Stuffing; Password list attack; Password re-use; Stolen credentials; Use of stolen credentials

SEE ALSO

- OAT-007 Credential Cracking
- OAT-019 Account Creation

CAPEC Category / Attack Pattern IDs

- 210 Abuse of Functionality

WASC Threat IDs

- 21 Insufficient Anti-Automation
- 42 Abuse of Functionality

CWEs

- 799 Improper Control of Interaction Frequency
- 837 Improper Enforcement of a Single, Unique Action

OWASP Attacks

- Abuse of Functionality
- Credential Stuffing

v1.2

OWASP Automated Threat Handbook Web Applications

Credential Stuffing OAT-008

Mass log in attempts used to verify the validity of stolen username/password pairs.

POSSIBLE SYMPTOMS

- Sequential login attempts with different credentials from the same HTTP client (based on IP, User Agent, device, fingerprint, patterns in HTTP headers, etc.)
- High number of failed login attempts
- Increased customer complaints of account hijacking through help center or social media outlets

SUGGESTED THREAT-SPECIFIC COUNTERMEASURES

Class	Threat-Specific Comments
Value	Consider providing guidance and encouragement to users about how to select stronger and unique passwords, and the importance of protecting relevant password recovery mechanisms (e.g. email account, mobile phones).
Requirements	Document acceptable use of authentication functions; define additional requirements.
Testing	Define test cases for **OAT-008 Credential Stuffing** that confirm the application will detect and/or prevent users attempting to use account credentials in bulk.
Capacity	Not applicable
Obfuscation	Consider randomising the content and URLs of authentication form pages, tying these changes to the individual user's session, verifying the changes at each authentication step, and restricting any identified automated usage.
Fingerprinting	Consider identifying and restricting automated usage by fingerprinting the User Agent for its unique characteristics.
Reputation	Consider identifying and restricting automated usage by reputation methods. In particular, consider using public breach data to identify at-risk user accounts and force a password change, or increase anti-fraud measures on these accounts. Consider using geolocation and/or IP address block lists to prevent access to authentication functions. Consider using email address reputation services, if used for username.
Authentication	Consider not permitting social media login. Consider methods to attempt to ensure users have unique passwords such as expiring passwords periodically and preventing password re-use. Consider enhancing authentication by adding CAPTCHA, or adding application-specific challenge questions, or using strong authentication such as two factor authentication. Consider preventing users from utilising email addresses as usernames, or using application-specific usernames which are less likely to exist on other systems. Consider stricter measures for user accounts with greater permissions (e.g. staff, moderators, content administrators, system accounts). Consider pre-registering users and implementing strong authentication for access to any exposed authentication APIs.
Rate	Limit the number of authentication attempts (success or failure) per session/user/IP address/device/fingerprint.
Monitoring	Log successful and unsuccessful authentication attempts across all functions (register, logon, password reset, password change, username change, re-authentication, etc) and channels (web, mobile app, call centre, etc); monitor rates relative to normal activity and also relative the usage of the rest of the application. Identify account hijacking reports from customers; monitor absolute numbers and trends.
Instrumentation	Consider blocking or delaying access by users in a particular session, IP address/range or geolocation or everyone once Monitoring has identified a real Credential Stuffing attack, or other anomalous behaviour that has identified the user as an attacker.
Contract	Define service limits for any authentication APIs.
Response	Define actions to be taken in the event a Credential Stuffing attack is detected.
Sharing	Participate in threat intelligence exchanges and contribute Credential Stuffing attack data to sector-wide sharing systems.

See also OWASP's Credential Stuffing Prevention Cheat Sheet at
https://www.owasp.org/index.php/Credential_Stuffing_Prevention_Cheat_Sheet

Automated Threat Event Reference

OAT-009

CAPTCHA Defeat

Solve anti-automation tests.

SECTORS TARGETED

Education
Entertainment
Financial
Government
Health
Retail
Technology
Social Networking

PARTIES AFFECTED

Few Individual Users
Many Users
Application Owner
Third Parties
Society

DATA COMMONLY MISUSED

Authentication Credentials
Payment Cardholder Data
Other Financial Data
Medical Data
Other Personal Data
Intellectual Property
Other Business Data
Public Information

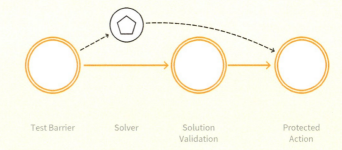

Test Barrier   Solver   Solution Validation   Protected Action

DESCRIPTION

Completely Automated Public Turing test to tell Computers and Humans Apart (CAPTCHA) challenges are used to distinguish normal users from bots. Automation is used in an attempt to analyse and determine the answer to visual and/or aural CAPTCHA tests and related puzzles. Apart from conventional visual and aural CAPTCHA, puzzle solving mini games or arithmetical exercises are sometimes used. Some of these may include context-specific challenges.

The process that determines the answer may utilise tools to perform optical character recognition, or matching against a prepared database of pre-generated images, or using other machine reading, or human farms.

OTHER NAMES AND EXAMPLES

Breaking CAPTCHA; CAPTCHA breaker; CAPTCHA breaking; CAPTCHA bypass; CAPTCHA decoding; CAPTCHA solver; CAPTCHA solving; Puzzle solving

SEE ALSO

- OAT-006 Expediting
- OAT-011 Scraping

CAPEC CATEGORY / ATTACK PATTERN IDs

-

WASC THREAT IDs

- 21 Insufficient Anti-Automation
- 42 Abuse of Functionality

CWEs

- 804 Guessable CAPTCHA
- 841 Improper Enforcement of Behavioral Workflow

OWASP ATTACKS

-

v1.2

OWASP Automated Threat Handbook Web Applications

CAPTCHA Defeat OAT-009

Solve anti-automation tests.

PossIBLE SYMPTOMS
- High CAPTCHA solving success rate on fraudulent accounts
- Suspiciously fast or fixed CAPTCHA solving times

SUGGESTED THREAT-SPECIFIC COUNTERMEASURES

Class	Threat-Specific Comments
Value	Not applicable
Requirements	Document acceptable use of CAPTCHA; define additional requirements.
Testing	Define test cases for **OAT-009 CAPTCHA Defeat** that confirm the application will detect and/or prevent users attempting to automate CAPTCHA breaking/solving.
Capacity	Not applicable
Obfuscation	Consider randomising the content and URLs of forms including CAPTCHA elements, tying these changes to the individual user's session, verifying the changes at each request, and restricting any identified automated usage.
Fingerprinting	Consider identifying and restricting automated usage by fingerprinting the User Agent for its unique characteristics.
Reputation	Consider identifying and restricting automated usage by reputation methods.
Authentication	Consider increasing CAPTCHA complexity. Consider replacing CAPTCHA with some form of identity authentication or require re-authentication.
Rate	Consider capping the rate of CAPTCHA verification per session/user/IP address/device/fingerprint.
Monitoring	Log CAPTCHA generation and solution speed and usage; monitor rate of use relative to typical usage. Correlate CAPTCHA solving rate against other indicators of suspicious/fraudulent account usage.
Instrumentation	Consider blocking or delaying access or delaying access by users in a particular session, IP address/range or geolocation once Monitoring has identified a real CAPTCHA Defeat attack, or other anomalous behaviour that has identified the user as an attacker.
Contract	Define T&Cs to explicitly define acceptable use.
Response	Define actions to be taken in the event a CAPTCHA Defeat attack is detected.
Sharing	Not applicable

Automated Threat Event Reference

OAT-010 Card Cracking

Identify missing start/expiry dates and security codes for stolen payment card data by trying different values.

SECTORS TARGETED
Education
Entertainment
Financial
Government
Health
Retail
Technology
Social Networking

PARTIES AFFECTED
Few Individual Users
Many Users
Application Owner
Third Parties
Society

DATA COMMONLY MISUSED
Authentication Credentials
Payment Cardholder Data
Other Financial Data
Medical Data
Other Personal Data
Intellectual Property
Other Business Data
Public Information

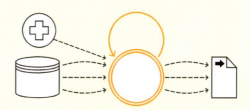

Stolen Partial Cardholder Data & Brute Forcing → Card Payment Process → Complete Cardholder Data

DESCRIPTION

Brute force attack against application payment card processes to identify the missing values for start date, expiry date and/or card security code (CSC), also referred to in many ways, including card validation number 2 (CVN2), card validation code (CVC), card verification value (CV2) and card identification number (CID).

When these values are known as well as the Primary Account Number (PAN), **OAT-001 Carding** is used to validate the details, and **OAT-012 Cashing Out** to obtain goods or cash.

OTHER NAMES AND EXAMPLES

Brute forcing credit card information; Card brute forcing; Credit card cracking; Distributed guessing attack

SEE ALSO

- OAT-001 Carding
- OAT-012 Cashing Out

CAPEC CATEGORY / ATTACK PATTERN IDs

- 112 Brute Force
- 210 Abuse of Functionality

WASC THREAT IDs

- 11 Brute Force
- 21 Insufficient Anti-Automation
- 42 Abuse of Functionality

CWEs

- 799 Improper Control of Interaction Frequency
- 837 Improper Enforcement of a Single, Unique Action

OWASP ATTACKS

- Abuse of Functionality
- Brute Force Attack

OWASP Automated Threat Handbook Web Applications

Card Cracking — OAT-010

Identify missing start/expiry dates and security codes for stolen payment card data by trying different values.

POSSIBLE SYMPTOMS

- Elevated basket abandonment
- Higher proportion of failed payment authorisations
- Disproportionate use of the payment step
- Reduced average basket price
- Increased chargebacks

SUGGESTED THREAT-SPECIFIC COUNTERMEASURES

Class	Threat-Specific Comments
Value	Consider fully outsourcing all payment aspects to an appropriate payment services provider (PSP) that has its own countermeasures in place for OAT-010. Increase the minimum checkout value. Consider removing payment by card completely if alternatives are available and suitable.
Requirements	Document acceptable use of checkout/payment functions; define additional requirements.
Testing	Define test cases for **OAT-010 Card Cracking** that confirm the application will detect and/or prevent users trying to guess start/expiry dates or security codes for a single payment card primary account number (PAN), and users trying multiple card PANs with a single expiry date and/or security code.
Capacity	Not applicable
Obfuscation	Consider randomising the content and URLs of payment form and payment submission pages, tying these changes to the individual user's session, verifying the changes at each payment step, and restricting any identified automated usage.
Fingerprinting	Consider identifying and restricting automated usage by fingerprinting the User Agent for its unique characteristics.
Reputation	Consider identifying and restricting automated usage by reputation methods. In particular, consider using geolocation and/or IP address block lists to prevent access to payment parts of the application. Consider using address and card reputation services. Consider adding delays in the checkout steps for new and/or infrequent customers, and for smaller checkout baskets, and for users that appear to have skipped directly to payment bypassing basket addition and checkout, or are using known fraudulent payment cards.
Authentication	Consider removing guest checkout and/or requiring greater identity authentication for customers. Consider adding CAPTCHA step for new and/or infrequent customers, and for smaller checkout baskets, and for users that appear to have skipped directly to payment. Consider implementing 3D Secure for some or all card payments. Consider pre-registering users and implementing strong authentication for access to any exposed payment APIs.
Rate	Consider limiting the number of failed card authorisation attempts per session/user/IP address/device/fingerprint.
Monitoring	Log abandoned baskets; monitor rates. Log basket payment amount (and currency); monitor average value trends. Log successful and failed card authorisations; monitor rates relative to normal activity and also relative the usage of the rest of the application. Track chargeback amounts and trends.
Instrumentation	Consider blocking or delaying payment function access by users in a particular session, IP address/range or geolocation or everyone once Monitoring has identified a real Card Cracking attack, or other anomalous behaviour that has identified the user as an attacker.
Contract	Define T&Cs to explicitly ban users from using the payment parts of the application to undertake Card Cracking, and consider requiring opt-in agreement to these before the application can be used (or as part of the checkout process). Define service limits for any payment APIs.
Response	Define actions to be taken in the event a Card Cracking attack is detected.
Sharing	Use card issuers' services that can identify distributed guessing attacks. Participate in e-commerce threat intelligence exchanges and contribute attack data to sector-wide sharing systems. Participate in any fraud detection and prevention arrangements offered by the payment service provider or merchant bank.

OAT-011

Automated Threat Event Reference

Scraping

Collect application content and/or other data for use elsewhere.

Sectors Targeted

Education

Entertainment

Financial

Government

Health

Retail

Technology

Social Networking

Parties Affected

Few Individual Users

Many Users

Application Owner

Third Parties

Society

Data Commonly Misused

Authentication Credentials

Payment Cardholder Data

Other Financial Data

Medical Data

Other Personal Data

Intellectual Property

Other Business Data

Public Information

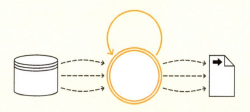

Target URL(s) and Parameter Values · Processes · Extracted Content and/or Data

Description

Collecting accessible data and/or processed output from the application. Some scraping may use fake or compromised accounts, or the information may be accessible without authentication. The scraper may attempt to read all accessible paths and parameter values for web pages and APIs, collecting the responses and extracting data from them. Scraping may occur in real time, or be more periodic in nature. Some Scraping may be used to gain insight into how it is constructed and operates - perhaps for cryptanalysis, reverse engineering, or session analysis.

When another application is being used as an intermediary between the user(s) and the real application, see **OAT-020 Account Aggregation**. If the intent is to obtain cash or goods, see **OAT-012 Cashing Out** instead.

Other Names and Examples

API provisioning; Bargain hunting; Comparative shopping; Content scraping; Data aggregation; Database scraping; Farming; Harvesting; Meta search scraper; Mining; Mirroring; Pagejacking; Powering APIs; Ripping; Scraper bot; Screen scraping; Search / social media bot

See Also

- OAT-012 Cashing Out
- OAT-018 Footprinting
- OAT-020 Account Aggregation

CAPEC Category / Attack Pattern IDs

- 167 Lifting Sensitive Data from the Client
- 210 Abuse of Functionality
- 281 Analyze Target

WASC Threat IDs

- 21 Insufficient Anti-Automation
- 42 Abuse of Functionality

CWEs

- 799 Improper Control of Interaction Frequency

OWASP Attacks

- Abuse of Functionality

v1.2

Scraping

OAT-011

Collect application content and/or other data for use elsewhere.

Possible Symptoms

- Unusual request activity for selected resources (e.g. high rate, high number, fixed period)
- Duplicated content from multiple sources in search engine results
- Decreased search engine ranking
- Increased network bandwidth usage with throughput problems
- New competitors with similar service offerings

Suggested Threat-Specific Countermeasures

Class	Threat-Specific Comments
Value	Consider using aggregation, and/or anonymisation and/or pseudonymisation. Consider data minimisation such as reducing the data fields collected and subsequently output, and/or reducing the retention period, permanent deletion of data no longer required. Consider outputting truncated, masked, abbreviated or encrypted data. Consider penalising access to data.
Requirements	Document what is acceptable usage and what is unacceptable scraping; define additional requirements.
Testing	Define test cases for **OAT-011 Scraping** that confirm the application will detect and/or prevent users attempting to scrape content and/or other data.
Capacity	Not applicable
Obfuscation	Consider randomising the content and URLs of content, tying these changes to the individual user's session, verifying the changes at each request, and restricting any identified automated usage.
Fingerprinting	Consider identifying and restricting automated usage by fingerprinting the User Agent for its unique characteristics.
Reputation	Consider identifying and restricting automated usage by fingerprinting the User Agent for its unique characteristics.
Authentication	Consider requiring greater identity authentication for access. Consider pre-registering users and implementing strong authentication for access to any exposed APIs.
Rate	Consider adding random delays in responses. Consider capping rate of application use per session/user/IP address/device/fingerprint.
Monitoring	Log request timestamps and rate of data access; monitor for faster-than-average access, repeated access, and non-normal access patterns.
Instrumentation	Consider blocking or delaying access or delaying access by users in a particular session, IP address/range or geolocation once Monitoring has identified a real Scraping attack, or other anomalous behaviour that has identified the user as an attacker.
Contract	Define T&Cs to explicitly define acceptable use that excludes Scraping.
Response	Define actions to be taken in the event a Scraping attack is detected.
Sharing	Participate in threat intelligence exchanges and contribute attack data to sector-wide sharing systems.

Note that in certain applications, some types of Scraping may be desirable, or even encouraged, rather than being threats.

Automated Threat Event Reference

OAT-012

Cashing Out

Buy goods or obtain cash utilising validated stolen payment card or other user account data.

SECTORS TARGETED

Education

Entertainment

Financial

Government

Health

Retail

Technology

Social Networking

PARTIES AFFECTED

Few Individual Users

Many Users

Application Owner

Third Parties

Society

DATA COMMONLY MISUSED

Authentication Credentials

Payment Cardholder Data

Other Financial Data

Medical Data

Other Personal Data

Intellectual Property

Other Business Data

Public Information

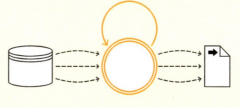

Stolen Payment Cardholder Data or Other User Account Data

Card Payment Process

Goods or Cash

DESCRIPTION

Obtaining currency or higher-value merchandise via the application using stolen, previously validated payment cards or other account login credentials. Cashing Out sometimes may be undertaken in conjunction with product return fraud. For financial transactions, this is usually a transfer of funds to a mule's account. For payment cards, this activity may occur following **OAT-001 Carding** of bulk stolen data, or **OAT-010 Card Cracking**, and the goods are dropped at a reshipper's address. The refunding of payments via non-financial applications (e.g. tax refunds, claims payment) is also included in Cashing Out.

Obtaining other information of value from the application is instead **OAT-011 Scraping**.

OTHER NAMES AND EXAMPLES

Deetsing; Money laundering; Online credit card fraud; Online payment card fraud; Refund fraud; Stolen identity refund fraud (SIRF)

SEE ALSO

- OAT-001 Carding
- OAT-011 Scraping
- OAT-010 Card Cracking

CAPEC CATEGORY / ATTACK PATTERN IDS

- 210 Abuse of Functionality

WASC THREAT IDS

- 21 Insufficient Anti-Automation
- 42 Abuse of Functionality

CWEs

- 799 Improper Control of Interaction Frequency
- 837 Improper Enforcement of a Single, Unique Action

OWASP ATTACKS

- Abuse of Functionality

OWASP Automated Threat Handbook Web Applications

Cashing Out   OAT-012

Buy goods or obtain cash utilising validated stolen payment card or other user account data.

POSSIBLE SYMPTOMS

- Increased chargebacks
- Increased usage of interlinked accounts (e.g. same phone number, same password, same or similar email address)
- Same or similar accounts for both "buyer" and "seller" in sites that facilitate consumer-to-consumer (C2C) commerce
- Increased demand for higher-value goods or services
- Increased demand for a single supplier's goods or services

SUGGESTED THREAT-SPECIFIC COUNTERMEASURES

Class	Threat-Specific Comments
Value	Decrease the number of and/or availability of higher-value items.
Requirements	Document acceptable use of relevant functions (e.g. payment, refund); define additional requirements.
Testing	Define test cases for **OAT-012 Cashing Out** that confirm the application will detect and/or prevent users attempting to cash out.
Capacity	Not applicable
Obfuscation	Consider randomising the content and URLs of relevant pages, tying these changes to the individual user's session, verifying the changes at each request, and restricting any identified automated usage.
Fingerprinting	Consider identifying and restricting automated usage by fingerprinting the User Agent for its unique characteristics.
Reputation	Consider identifying and restricting automated usage by reputation methods. In particular, consider using geolocation and/or IP address block lists to prevent access to relevant parts of the application.
Authentication	Consider removing guest checkout and/or requiring greater identity authentication for customers. Consider implementing 3D Secure for some or all card payments. Consider requiring increased verification and out-of-band confirmation of all changes to account properties (e.g. email addresses, telephone numbers, physical addresses, bank accounts).
Rate	Consider limiting the number of payments/transactions per session/user/IP address/device/fingerprint.
Monitoring	Log abandoned baskets/transactions; monitor rates. Log basket/transaction payment amount (and currency); monitor average value trends. Identify and log higher-value transactions. Log changes to asset destination (e.g. delivery addresses, recipient bank account); monitor activity related to transactions occurring soon after such events have occurred. Track chargeback and returns amounts and trends.
Instrumentation	Consider blocking or delaying access or delaying access by users in a particular session, IP address/range or geolocation once Monitoring has identified a real Cashing Out attack, or other anomalous behaviour that has identified the user as an attacker.
Contract	Not applicable
Response	Define actions to be taken in the event a Cashing Out attack is detected.
Sharing	Participate in threat intelligence exchanges and contribute attack data to sector-wide sharing systems. Participate in any fraud detection and prevention arrangements offered by the payment service provider or merchant bank.

OAT-013

Automated Threat Event Reference

Sniping

Last minute bid or offer for goods or services.

SECTORS TARGETED
Education
Entertainment
Financial
Government
Health
Retail
Technology
Social Networking

PARTIES AFFECTED
Few Individual Users
Many Users
Application Owner
Third Parties
Society

DATA COMMONLY MISUSED
Authentication Credentials
Payment Cardholder Data
Other Financial Data
Medical Data
Other Personal Data
Intellectual Property
Other Business Data
Public Information

Monitoring For Opportunity → Bid or Offer Process → Acquired Asset Identity

DESCRIPTION

The defining characteristic of Sniping is an action undertaken at the latest opportunity to achieve a particular objective, leaving insufficient time for another user to bid/offer. Sniping can also be the automated exploitation of system latencies in the form of timing attacks. Careful timing and prompt action are necessary parts. It is most well known as auction sniping, but the same threat event can be used in other types of applications. Sniping normally leads to some disbenefit for other users, and sometimes that might be considered a form of denial of service.

In contrast, **OAT-005 Scalping** is the acquisition of limited availability of sought-after goods or services, and **OAT-006 Expediting** is the general hastening of progress.

OTHER NAMES AND EXAMPLES

Auction sniping; Bid sniper; Front-running; Last look; Last minute bet; Timing attack

SEE ALSO

- OAT-005 Scalping
- OAT-006 Expediting
- OAT-015 Denial of Service
- OAT-021 Denial of Inventory

CAPEC CATEGORY / ATTACK PATTERN IDs

- 210 Abuse of Functionality

WASC THREAT IDs

- 21 Insufficient Anti-Automation
- 42 Abuse of Functionality

CWEs

-

OWASP ATTACKS

- Abuse of Functionality

… OWASP Automated Threat Handbook Web Applications

Sniping

OAT-013

Last minute bid or offer for goods or services.

POSSIBLE SYMPTOMS

- Increasing complaints from users about being unable to obtain goods/services
- Some users having greater success rate than expected

SUGGESTED THREAT-SPECIFIC COUNTERMEASURES

Class	Threat-Specific Comments
Value	Consider penalising later bets/bids/purchases, and/or encouraging earlier bets/bids/purchases.
Requirements	Document acceptable use of relevant functions (e.g. bet, bid, purchase); define additional requirements.
Testing	Define test cases for **OAT-013 Sniping** that confirm the application will detect and/or prevent users attempting to make last minute bids for goods or services.
Capacity	Not applicable
Obfuscation	Randomise the content and URLs, tying these changes to the individual user's session, verifying the changes at each request, and restricting any identified automated usage.
Fingerprinting	Consider identifying and restricting automated usage by fingerprinting the User Agent for its unique characteristics.
Reputation	Consider identifying and restricting automated usage by reputation methods. In particular, consider using geolocation and/or IP address block lists and/or reputation services to prevent access to the good/service allocation functions.
Authentication	Consider requiring identity authentication, re-authentication or some other increased authentication assurance for access to relevant processes for all users, or when there is a suspicion that Sniping is occurring.
Rate	Consider not publishing or increasing uncertainty in the final closing time for bets/bids/purchase.
Monitoring	Log process step completion timestamps and rate of data entry; monitor for bypassing of earlier steps and/or longer-than-usual delays in completing final step. Log successful and unsuccessful bets/bids/purchases; monitor for unusual trends or and higher-than-normal success rate.
Instrumentation	Consider blocking or delaying access or delaying access by users in a particular session, IP address/range or geolocation once Monitoring has identified a real Sniping attack, or other anomalous behaviour that has identified the user as an attacker.
Contract	Define T&Cs to explicitly define acceptable use.
Response	Define actions to be taken in the event a Sniping attack is detected.
Sharing	Participate in threat intelligence exchanges and contribute Sniping attack data to sector-wide sharing systems.

Automated Threat Event Reference

OAT-014 Vulnerability Scanning

Crawl and fuzz application to identify weaknesses and possible vulnerabilities.

SECTORS TARGETED

Education

Entertainment

Financial

Government

Health

Retail

Technology

Social Networking

PARTIES AFFECTED

Few Individual Users

Many Users

Application Owner

Third Parties

Society

DATA COMMONLY MISUSED

Authentication Credentials

Payment Cardholder Data

Other Financial Data

Medical Data

Other Personal Data

Intellectual Property

Other Business Data

Public Information

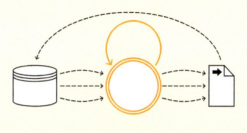

Target URL(s), Parameters & Payloads — Processes — Vulnerabilities

DESCRIPTION

Systematic enumeration and examination of identifiable, guessable and unknown content locations, paths, file names, parameters, in order to find weaknesses and points where a security vulnerability might exist. Vulnerability Scanning includes both malicious scanning and friendly scanning by an authorised vulnerability scanning engine. It differs from **OAT-011 Scraping** in that its aim is to identify potential vulnerabilities.

The exploitation of individual vulnerabilities is not included in the scope of this ontology, but this process of scanning, along with **OAT-018 Footprinting**, OAT-004 Fingerprinting and **OAT-011 Scraping** often form part of application penetration testing.

OTHER NAMES AND EXAMPLES

Active/Passive scanning; Application-specific vulnerability discovery; Identifying vulnerable content management systems (CMS) and CMS components; Known vulnerability scanning; Malicious crawling; Vulnerability reconnaissance

SEE ALSO

- OAT-004 Fingerprinting
- OAT-011 Scraping
- OAT-018 Footprinting

CAPEC CATEGORY / ATTACK PATTERN IDs

-

WASC THREAT IDs

- 21 Insufficient Anti-Automation

CWEs

- 799 Improper Control of Interaction Frequency

OWASP ATTACKS

-

OWASP Automated Threat Handbook Web Applications

Vulnerability Scanning   OAT-014

Crawl and fuzz application to identify weaknesses and possible vulnerabilities.

Possible Symptoms

- Highly elevated occurrence of errors (e.g. HTTP status code 404 not found, data validation failures, authorisation failures)
- Extremely high application usage from a single IP address
- Exotic value for HTTP user agent header
- High ratio of GET/POST to HEAD requests for a user/session/IP address compared to typical users
- Low ratio of static to dynamic content requests for a user/session/IP address compared to typical users
- Multiple misuse attempts against application entry points
- Parameter/header fuzzing

Suggested Threat-Specific Countermeasures

Class	Threat-Specific Comments
Value	Develop and deploy applications securely, identify and fix security issues as soon and quickly as possible.
Requirements	Not applicable
Testing	Define test cases for **OAT-014 Vulnerability Scanning** that confirm the application will detect and/or prevent users scanning it for vulnerabilities.
Capacity	Not applicable
Obfuscation	Consider making the application behaviour and/or structure so that vulnerability scanners/crawlers/testers are seemingly unable to ever complete a full site scan and/or unable to access some parts of an application.
Fingerprinting	Consider identifying and restricting automated usage by fingerprinting the User Agent for its unique characteristics.
Reputation	Consider denying or restricting access from IP addresses known to be vulnerability scanners or cloud providers.
Authentication	Consider requiring normal or strong authentication for some or all parts of the application. Consider requiring periodic and/or aspect-based reauthentication.
Rate	Limit the number of input validation and/or authorisation failures per session/user/IP address/device/fingerprint.
Monitoring	Log successful and failed authentications, authorisation failures, input validation failures; monitor rates relative to normal activity and also relative the usage of the rest of the application.
Instrumentation	Implement user and system wide trend detection points together with request, input validation and authorisation detection points. Consider blocking users or logging them out for non-normal use of the application.
Contract	Define T&Cs to explicitly ban users from scanning the application for vulnerabilities, and consider requiring opt-in agreement to these before the application can be use. Define approved methods of engagement for authorised vulnerability scanning.
Response	Define actions to be taken in the event a Vulnerability Scanning attack is detected.
Sharing	Participate in relevant threat intelligence sharing initiatives.

Automated Threat Event Reference

OAT-015

Denial of Service

Target resources of the application and database servers, or individual user accounts, to achieve denial of service (DoS).

SECTORS TARGETED

Education

Entertainment

Financial

Government

Health

Retail

Technology

Social Networking

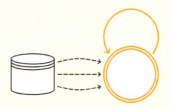

Target URL(s) and Parameter Values

Process(es)

PARTIES AFFECTED

Few Individual Users

Many Users

Application Owner

Third Parties

Society

DATA COMMONLY MISUSED

Authentication Credentials

Payment Cardholder Data

Other Financial Data

Medical Data

Other Personal Data

Intellectual Property

Other Business Data

Public Information

DESCRIPTION

Usage may resemble legitimate application usage, but leads to exhaustion of resources such as file system, memory, processes, threads, CPU, and human or financial resources. The resources might be related to web, application or databases servers or other services supporting the application, such as third party APIs, included third-party hosted content, or content delivery networks (CDNs). The application may be affected as a whole, or the attack may be against individual users such as account lockout.

This ontology's scope excludes other forms of denial of service that affect web applications, namely HTTP Flood DoS (GET, POST, Header with/without TLS), HTTP Slow DoS, IP layer 3 DoS, and TCP layer 4 DoS. Those protocol and lower layer aspects are covered adequately in other taxonomies and lists.

OTHER NAMES AND EXAMPLES

Account lockout; App layer DDoS; Asymmetric resource consumption (amplification); Business logic DDoS; Cash overflow; Forced deadlock; Hash DoS; Inefficient code; Indexer DoS; Large files DoS; Resource depletion, locking or exhaustion; Sustained client engagement

SEE ALSO

- OAT-005 Scalping
- OAT-013 Sniping
- OAT-017 Spamming
- OAT-019 Account Creation
- OAT-021 Denial of Inventory

CAPEC CATEGORY / ATTACK PATTERN IDS

- 2 Inducing Account Lockout
- 25 Forced Deadlock
- 119 Deplete Resources

WASC THREAT IDS

- 10 Denial of Service

CWEs

- 399 Resource Management Errors
- 645 Overly Restrictive Account Lockout Mechanism

OWASP ATTACKS

- Account Lockout Attack
- Cash Overflow
- Denial of Service
- Resource Depletion

OWASP Automated Threat Handbook Web Applications

Denial of Service — OAT-015

Target resources of the application and database servers, or individual user accounts, to achieve denial of service (DoS).

Possible Symptoms

- Spikes in CPU, memory and network utilization
- Unavailability of part or all of the application
- Rise in user account lockouts
- Rise is complaints about poor performance
- Reduced website performance and service degradation

Suggested Threat-Specific Countermeasures

Class	Threat-Specific Comments
Value	Consider reducing and/or eliminating resource intensive functionality, or using alternatives.
Requirements	Document average and peak (at different durations) usage of all functions and paths, including APIs, included content and third-party components and services, for all types of permitted automated robot activity as well as normal user usage during standard, seasonal, and other relevant scenarios. Define additional requirements.
Testing	Define test cases for **OAT-015 Denial of Service** that confirm the application will detect and/or prevent users performing application denial of service. These test cases should include attacks against particularly susceptible functions, against user accounts, or against other application system resources.
Capacity	Identify all capacity pinch points, for both normal and peak usage. Provide adequate greater capacity for system components based on risk. This may include providing specific API or data feeds for data provision, application configuration, SSL configuration, designing lowly-loaded systems, load balancing, auto-scaling, caching, content delivery networks, SSL accelerators/terminators, XML gateways, content switching, query caching, query optimisation, application delivery controller, denial of service (DoS) protection service, etc.
Obfuscation	Not applicable
Fingerprinting	Consider identifying and restricting automated usage by fingerprinting the User Agent for its unique characteristics.
Reputation	Consider identifying and restricting automated usage by reputation methods.
Authentication	Consider requiring authentication or enhanced authentication for high resource usage aspects of the application.
Rate	Consider limiting availability and/or rate of usage of high resource usage aspects of the application.
Monitoring	Log application site usage, account lockout, product/service availability, critical resource usage, etc; monitor against multiple alerting thresholds as well as changes to trends.
Instrumentation	Consider blocking or delaying application access by individual users or groups of users based on behaviour and/or session, and/or IP address/range and/or geolocation once Monitoring has identified a real Denial of Service attack, or other anomalous behaviour that has identified the user(s) as an attacker(s). Consider disabling at resource intensive functions progressively to maintain availability of other aspects.
Contract	Define acceptable use and service limits for the application, including any APIs and related components.
Response	Define actions to be taken in the event a Denial of Service attack is detected.
Sharing	Participate in threat intelligence exchanges and contribute Denial of Service attack data to sector-wide sharing systems.

Note that web application denial of service can often be the side effect of some other web application automated threat. Separately, non web application denial of service such as network, HTTP and SSL/TLS may also occur.

Automated Threat Event Reference

OAT-016

Skewing

Repeated link clicks, page requests or form submissions intended to alter some metric.

Sectors Targeted

Education

Entertainment

Financial

Government

Health

Retail

Technology

Social Networking

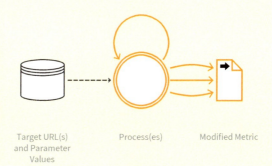

Target URL(s) and Parameter Values

Process(es)

Modified Metric

Parties Affected

Few Individual Users

Many Users

Application Owner

Third Parties

Society

Description

Automated repeated clicking or requesting or submitting content, affecting application-based metrics such as counts and measures of frequency and/or rate. The metric or measurement may be visible to users (e.g. betting odds, likes, market/dynamic pricing, visitor count, poll results, reviews) or hidden (e.g. application usage statistics, business performance indicators). Metrics may affect individuals as well as the application owner, e.g. user reputation, influence others, gain fame, or undermine someone else's reputation.

For malicious alteration of digital advertisement metrics, see **OAT-003 Ad Fraud** instead.

Data Commonly Misused

Authentication Credentials

Payment Cardholder Data

Other Financial Data

Medical Data

Other Personal Data

Intellectual Property

Other Business Data

Public Information

Other Names and Examples

Biasing KPIs; Boosting friends, visitors, and likes; Click fraud; Dynamic pricing hacking; Election fraud; Hit count fraud; Market distortion; Metric and statistic skewing; Page impression fraud; Poll fraud; Poll skewing; Poll/voting subversion; Rating/review skewing; SEO; Stock manipulation; Survey skewing

See Also

- OAT-003 Ad Fraud
- OAT-017 Spamming
- OAT-019 Account Creation

CAPEC Category / Attack Pattern IDs

- 210 Abuse of Functionality

WASC Threat IDs

- 21 Insufficient Anti-Automation
- 42 Abuse of Functionality

CWEs

- 799 Improper Control of Interaction Frequency
- 837 Improper Enforcement of a Single, Unique Action

OWASP Attacks

- Abuse of Functionality

v1.2

OWASP Automated Threat Handbook Web Applications

Skewing   OAT-016

Repeated link clicks, page requests or form submissions intended to alter some metric.

Possible Symptoms

- Decreased click/impression to outcome ratio (e.g. check out, conversion)
- Unexpected or unexplained changes to a metric
- Metric significantly different to accepted sector norms
- Increased costs/awards that are determined from an application metric or metrics

Suggested Threat-Specific Countermeasures

Class	Threat-Specific Comments
Value	Not applicable
Requirements	Identify all metrics and ways they could be manipulated by different types of users; define additional requirements. Define logging requirements that capture sufficient information for thorough analysis of application activity contributing to each metric.
Testing	Define test cases for **OAT-016 Skewing** that confirm the application will detect and/or prevent users attempting to skew metrics.
Capacity	Not applicable
Obfuscation	Consider randomising the content and URLs of metric-related content, tying these changes to the individual user's session, verifying the changes at each request, and restricting any identified automated usage.
Fingerprinting	Consider identifying and restricting automated usage by fingerprinting the User Agent for its unique characteristics. Use the information to reject related metric contributions.
Reputation	Consider identifying and restricting automated usage by reputation methods. In particular, consider using geolocation and/or IP address block lists and/or reputation services to exclude fraudulent data contributing to the metrics.
Authentication	Consider requiring identity authentication, re-authentication or some other increased authentication assurance for access to areas where metric data are collected.
Rate	Consider adding delays to metric-contributing actions. Consider limiting the number of times and/or rate at which the activity of a session, and/or IP address, and/or account/user and/or device/fingerprint contributes to each metric. Consider enforcing single-use and a limited period of validity for metric-contributing one-time tokens/codes.
Monitoring	Log all activity contributing to metrics; monitor trends and abnormal patterns. Perform analysis, near real-time if possible, for common patterns in users' system fingerprints, IP addresses and HTTP headers (such as User Agent, cookies, etc.), especially for requests during extremes of metric values.
Instrumentation	Not applicable
Contract	Define end user T&Cs, employee contracts, corporate policies etc to ensure users understand that metric Skewing is not permissible.
Response	Define actions to be taken in the event a Skewing attack is detected.
Sharing	Not applicable

Note that a significant change to a metric may actually be real, and not the result of an automated threat event. Skewing could also be the side effect of some other automated threat

Automated Threat Event Reference

OAT-017

Spamming

Malicious or questionable information addition that appears in public or private content, databases or user messages.

SECTORS TARGETED

Education

Entertainment

Financial

Government

Health

Retail

Technology

Social Networking

PARTIES AFFECTED

Few Individual Users

Many Users

Application Owner

Third Parties

Society

DATA COMMONLY MISUSED

Authentication Credentials

Payment Cardholder Data

Other Financial Data

Medical Data

Other Personal Data

Intellectual Property

Other Business Data

Public Information

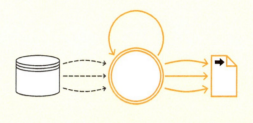

Target URL(s) and Parameter Values — Process(es) — Stored & Transmitted Spam Content

DESCRIPTION

Malicious content can include malware, IFRAME distribution, photographs & videos, advertisements, referrer spam and tracking/surveillance code. The content might be less overtly malicious but be an attempt to cause mischief, undertake search engine optimisation (SEO) or to dilute/hide other posts.

The mass abuse of broken form-to-email and form-to-SMS functions to send messages to unintended recipients is not included in this threat event, or any other in this ontology, since those are considered to be the exploitation of implementation flaws alone.

For multiple use that distorts metrics, see **OAT-016 Skewing** instead.

OTHER NAMES AND EXAMPLES

Blog spam; Bulletin board spam; Click-bait; Comment spam; Content spam; Content spoofing; Fake news; Form spam; Forum spam; Guestbook spam; Referrer spam; Review spam; SEO spam; Spam crawlers; Spam 2.0; Spambot; Twitter spam; Wiki spam

SEE ALSO

- OAT-015 Denial of Service
- OAT-016 Skewing
- OAT-019 Account Creation

CAPEC CATEGORY / ATTACK PATTERN IDs

- 210 Abuse of Functionality

WASC THREAT IDs

- 21 Insufficient Anti-Automation
- 42 Abuse of Functionality

CWEs

- 506 Embedded Malicious Code
- 799 Improper Control of Interaction Frequency
- 837 Improper Enforcement of a Single, Unique Action

OWASP ATTACKS

- Abuse of Functionality

v1.2

Spamming   OAT-017

Malicious or questionable information addition that appears in public or private content, databases or user messages.

Possible Symptoms

- Increase in the rejection rate of user-generated content by moderation processes
- Higher rate of complaints from users about spam content
- High appearance of typically fraudulent keyword in user-generated content (e.g. celebrity names, insurance, viagra)
- High hyperlink density
- Inclusion of hyperlinks to web hosts that redirect, or with low reputation, or that host malicious content directly
- Requests from source IP addresses, devices, fingerprints that appear on spam lists

Suggested Threat-Specific Countermeasures

Class	Threat-Specific Comments
Value	Consider ensuring there are frequent data backups so that original information and state can be restored in the event of contamination by a spamming attack. Consider limiting the functionality and/or capacity available to newly, or recently, created accounts. Consider preventing users from adding/sending URLs, and/or images, and/or other files.
Requirements	Identify all aspects of the application that could be used to generate spam; define additional requirements. Define logging requirements that capture sufficient information to assess whether spamming is occurring.
Testing	Define test cases for **OAT-017 Spamming** that confirm the application will detect and/or prevent users attempting to generate spam.
Capacity	Not applicable
Obfuscation	Consider randomising the content and URLs of content, tying these changes to the individual user's session, verifying the changes at each request, and restricting any identified automated usage.
Fingerprinting	Consider identifying and restricting automated usage by fingerprinting the User Agent for its unique characteristics.
Reputation	Consider denying or restricting access from IP addresses known to be vulnerability scanners, web crawlers or cloud providers."
Authentication	Consider requiring identity authentication, re-authentication or some other increased authentication assurance for access to areas where user-generated content, alerts or messages are created.
Rate	Consider adding delays to actions the create user-generated content, alerts or messages.
Monitoring	Consider the use of moderation for user-generated content. Log all activity related to functions that could be used to generate spam; monitor trends and abnormal patterns. Perform analysis, near real-time if possible, for common patterns in users' system fingerprints, IP addresses and HTTP headers (such as User Agent, cookies, etc.). Identify spam reports from customers; monitor trends.
Instrumentation	Consider blocking or delaying access or delaying access by users in a particular session, IP address/range or geolocation once Monitoring has identified a real Spamming attack, or other anomalous behaviour that has identified the user as an attacker.
Contract	Define end user T&Cs, employee contracts, corporate policies etc to ensure users understand that any form of Spamming is not permissible.
Response	Define actions to be taken in the event a Spamming attack is detected.
Sharing	Participate in threat intelligence exchanges and contribute Spamming attack data to sector-wide sharing systems.

Automated Threat Event Reference

OAT-018

Footprinting

Probe and explore application to identify its constituents and properties.

Sectors Targeted

Education

Entertainment

Financial

Government

Health

Retail

Technology

Social Networking

Target URL(s) and Parameters Values — Processes — Enumerated Application Details

Parties Affected

Few Individual Users

Many Users

Application Owner

Third Parties

Society

Data Commonly Misused

Authentication Credentials

Payment Cardholder Data

Other Financial Data

Medical Data

Other Personal Data

Intellectual Property

Other Business Data

Public Information

Description

Information gathering with the objective of learning as much as possible about the composition, configuration and security mechanisms of the application. Unlike Scraping, Footprinting is an enumeration of the application itself, rather than the data. It is used to identify all the URL paths, parameters and values, and process sequences (i.e. to determine entry points, also collectively called the attack surface). As the application is explored, additional paths will be identified which in turn need to be examined.

Footprinting can also include brute force, dictionary and guessing of file and directory names. Fuzzing may also be used to identify further application resources and capabilities. However, it does not include attempts to exploit weaknesses.

Other Names and Examples

Application analysis; API discovery; Application enumeration; Automated scanning; CGI scanning; Crawler; Crawling; Excavation; Forceful browsing; Forceful browsing; Fuzzing; Micro service discovery; Scanning; Spidering; WSDL scanning

See Also

- OAT-004 Fingerprinting
- OAT-011 Scraping

CAPEC Category / Attack Pattern IDs

- 169 Footprinting

WASC Threat IDs

- 45 Fingerprinting

CWEs

- 200 Information Exposure

OWASP Attacks

-

Footprinting

OAT-018

Probe and explore application to identify its constituents and properties.

Possible Symptoms

- Increase in system and application error codes, such as HTTP status codes 404 and 503, in the same user session
- Users that exercise the functionality of the entire application in manner that diverges from typical user behaviour

Suggested Threat-Specific Countermeasures

Class	Threat-Specific Comments
Value	Not applicable
Requirements	Not applicable
Testing	Not applicable
Capacity	Not applicable
Obfuscation	Consider randomising URLs. Consider preventing indexing by search engines. Consider minimising information leakage through HTTP errors, error messages, URL paths, and file extensions.
Fingerprinting	Consider identifying and restricting automated usage by fingerprinting the User Agent for its unique characteristics.
Reputation	Consider denying or restricting access from IP addresses known to be vulnerability scanners, web crawlers or cloud providers.
Authentication	Consider requiring normal or strong authentication for some or all parts of the application.
Rate	Consider adding time delays in responses or returning an error code such as 503 to higher usage user requests.
Monitoring	Not applicable
Instrumentation	Consider blocking users for non-normal use of the application. Consider honeypot detection points at URLs no normal users would ever navigate to.
Contract	Not applicable
Response	Not applicable
Sharing	Not applicable

Automated Threat Event Reference

OAT-019   Account Creation

Create multiple accounts for subsequent misuse.

SECTORS TARGETED

Education

Entertainment

Financial

Government

Health

Retail

Technology

Social Networking

PARTIES AFFECTED

Few Individual Users

Many Users

Application Owner

Third Parties

Society

DATA COMMONLY MISUSED

Authentication Credentials

Payment Cardholder Data

Other Financial Data

Medical Data

Other Personal Data

Intellectual Property

Other Business Data

Public Information

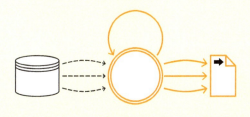

Identity Source Data   Registration/User Enrolment Process(es)   Created Accounts

DESCRIPTION

Bulk account creation, and sometimes profile population, by using the application's account sign-up processes. The accounts are subsequently misused for generating content spam, laundering cash and goods, spreading malware, affecting reputation, causing mischief, and skewing search engine optimisation (SEO), reviews and surveys.

Account Creation generates new accounts - see **OAT-007 Credential Cracking** and **OAT-008 Credential Stuffing** for threat events that use existing accounts.

OTHER NAMES AND EXAMPLES

Account pharming; Fake account; Fake social media account creation; Impersonator bot; Massive account registration; New account creation; Registering many user accounts

SEE ALSO

- OAT-007 Credential Cracking
- OAT-008 Credential Stuffing

CAPEC CATEGORY / ATTACK PATTERN IDs

- 210 Abuse of Functionality

WASC THREAT IDs

- 21 Insufficient Anti-Automation
- 42 Abuse of Functionality

CWEs

- 799 Improper Control of Interaction Frequency
- 837 Improper Enforcement of a Single, Unique Action
- 841 Improper Enforcement of Behavioral Workflow

OWASP ATTACKS

- Abuse of Functionality

v1.2

Account Creation OAT-019

Create multiple accounts for subsequent misuse.

POSSIBLE SYMPTOMS

- Higher than average account creation rate compared to average rate over time
- Accounts with incomplete information relative to the typical account holders
- Accounts created but which are not used immediately
- Accounts created with disproportionate use, and/or misuse, of the application's functionalities

SUGGESTED THREAT-SPECIFIC COUNTERMEASURES

Class	Threat-Specific Comments
Value	Consider limiting the functionality and/or capacity available to newly, and/or recently created, accounts.
Requirements	Document acceptable use of all possible account creation functions; define additional requirements.
Testing	Define test cases for **OAT-019 Account Creation** that confirm the application will detect and/or prevent users attempting to create accounts in bulk.
Capacity	Not applicable
Obfuscation	Consider randomising the content and URLs of account creation form pages, tying these changes to the individual user's session, verifying the changes at each request, and restricting any identified automated usage.
Fingerprinting	Consider identifying and restricting automated usage by fingerprinting the User Agent for its unique characteristics.
Reputation	Consider removing self-registration to existing known people (e.g. approved suppliers and/or customers). Consider identifying and restricting automated usage by reputation methods. In particular, consider using geolocation and/or IP address block lists to prevent access to registration/sign-up or to apply enhanced authentication requirements. Consider using reputation services (e.g. IP address, email address, postal address) to assist in
Authentication	Consider removing self-registration. Consider not permitting social media login. Consider out-of-band verification (e.g. email address verification). Consider enhancing authentication by adding CAPTCHA, or adding application-specific challenge questions, or using strong authentication such as two factor authentication. Consider pre-registering users and implementing strong authentication for access to any exposed authentication APIs.
Rate	Limit the rate of creation of accounts.
Monitoring	Log application usage by function for each user; monitor rate of application use relative to typical usage. Log account creation dates/times; monitor period from time of account creation to first use, and also monitor completeness of optional account information, and whether any profile text or images are generic, re-used or copied from elsewhere.
Instrumentation	Consider blocking or delaying access or delaying access by users in a particular session, IP address/range or geolocation or everyone once Monitoring has identified a real Account Creation attack, or other anomalous behaviour (possibly much later) that has identified the user as an attacker.
Contract	Define T&Cs to explicitly define acceptable use. Define service limits for any account creation APIs.
Response	Define actions to be taken in the event an Account Creation attack is detected.
Sharing	Participate in threat intelligence exchanges and contribute Account Creation attack data to sector-wide sharing systems.

Automated Threat Event Reference

OAT-020

Account Aggregation

Use by an intermediary application that collects together multiple accounts and interacts on their behalf.

Sectors Targeted
Education
Entertainment
Financial
Government
Health
Retail
Technology
Social Networking

Parties Affected
Few Individual Users
Many Users
Application Owner
Third Parties
Society

Data Commonly Misused
Authentication Credentials
Payment Cardholder Data
Other Financial Data
Medical Data
Other Personal Data
Intellectual Property
Other Business Data
Public Information

Intermediary Application Processes → Application Processes → Changed Data

Description
Compilation of credentials and information from multiple application accounts into another system. This aggregation application may be used by a single user to merge information from multiple applications, or alternatively to merge information of many users of a single application. Commonly used for aggregating social media accounts, email accounts and financial accounts in order to obtain a consolidated overview, to provide integrated reporting and analysis, and to simplify usage and consumption by the user and/or their professional advisors. May include making changes to account properties and interacting with the aggregated application's functionality.

For other forms of data harvesting, including the distribution of content, see **OAT-011 Scraping**. For hastening progress, see **OAT-006 Expediting** instead.

Other Names and Terms
Aggregator; Brokering; Client aggregator; Cloud services brokerage; Data aggregation; Financial account aggregator; Intermediarisation; Intermediation

See Also
- OAT-006 Expediting
- OAT-011 Scraping
- OAT-019 Account Creation

CAPEC Category / Attack Pattern IDs
- 167 Lifting Sensitive Data from the Client
- 210 Abuse of Functionality

WASC Threat IDs
- 21 Insufficient Anti-Automation
- 42 Abuse of Functionality

CWEs
- 799 Improper Control of Interaction Frequency

OWASP Attacks
- Abuse of Functionality

v1.2

… OWASP Automated Threat Handbook Web Applications

Account Aggregation — OAT-020

Use by an intermediary application that collects together multiple accounts and interacts on their behalf.

POSSIBLE SYMPTOMS

- Lack of end user engagement with the service provider
- Account information access behavior patterns (e.g. geolocation, time zones) that do not match the user profile
- Elevated activity peaks
- Account credentials identified elsewhere

SUGGESTED THREAT-SPECIFIC COUNTERMEASURES

Class	Threat-Specific Comments
Value	Consider providing dedicated APIs for any approved aggregators. Consider providing benefits to users that are using the application directly (and not via an account aggregator). Consider providing separate functionality for users' approved and authenticated advisors etc so they can view either individual client or aggregated client access.
Requirements	Identify where Account Aggregation would be a threat to the application; define additional requirements.
Testing	Define test cases for **OAT-020 Account Aggregation** that confirm the application will detect and/or prevent users utilising some form of aggregation.
Capacity	Not applicable
Obfuscation	Consider randomising the content and URLs of key content, tying these changes to the individual user's session, verifying the changes at each request, and restricting any identified automated usage.
Fingerprinting	Consider identifying and restricting automated usage by fingerprinting the User Agent for its unique characteristics.
Reputation	Consider identifying and restricting automated usage by reputation methods. In particular, consider identifying and blocking IP addresses of known aggregation services.
Authentication	Consider creating and enforcing password aging controls. Consider enhancing authentication by adding CAPTCHA, or adding application-specific challenge questions, or using strong authentication such as two factor authentication. Consider pre-registering users and implementing strong authentication for access to any exposed APIs. Consider implementing strong authentication application-wide.
Rate	Limit the rate of requests per session/user/IP address/device/fingerprint.
Monitoring	Log application-wide activity; monitor for unusual peaks. Log click-through and conversion rates for links within the application; monitor individual user rates relative to average rates. Log access behaviour patterns (e.g. source geolocation, days/times, paths taken by user through the application); monitor repeated patterns for individuals and groups of users.
Instrumentation	Consider blocking or delaying access by users in a particular session, IP address/range or geolocation once Monitoring has identified a real Account Aggregation attack, or other anomalous behaviour that has identified the user as an attacker.
Contract	Define T&Cs to explicitly ban users from using aggregation tools, and consider requiring opt-in agreement to these before the application can be used. Define acceptable use and service limits for any APIs used by approved aggregators.
Response	Define actions to be taken in the event an Account Aggregation attack is detected.
Sharing	Participate in threat intelligence exchanges and contribute Account Aggregation attack data to sector-wide sharing systems.

Note that in certain applications, some types of Account Aggregation may be desirable, or even encouraged, rather than being threats.

Automated Threat Event Reference

OAT-021
Denial of Inventory

Deplete goods or services stock without ever completing the purchase or committing to the transaction.

Sectors Targeted

Education
Entertainment
Financial
Government
Health
Retail
Technology
Social Networking

Parties Affected

Few Individual Users
Many Users
Application Owner
Third Parties
Society

Data Commonly Misused

Authentication Credentials
Payment Cardholder Data
Other Financial Data
Medical Data
Other Personal Data
Intellectual Property
Other Business Data
Public Information

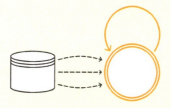

Target URL(s) and Parameter Values | Goods / Services Allocation Process(es) | Purchase / Commitment Process(es)

Description

Selection and holding of items from a limited inventory or stock, but which are never actually bought, or paid for, or confirmed, such that other users are unable to buy/pay/confirm the items themselves. It differs from **OAT-005 Scalping** in that the goods or services are never actually acquired by the attacker.

Denial of Inventory is most commonly thought of as taking ecommerce items out of circulation by adding many of them to a cart/basket; the attacker never actually proceeds to checkout to buy them but contributes to a possible stock-out condition. A variation of this automated threat event is making reservations (e.g. hotel rooms, restaurant tables, holiday bookings, flight seats), and/or click-and-collect without payment. But this exhaustion of inventory availability also occurs in other types of web application such as in the assignment of non-goods like service allocations, product rations, availability slots, queue positions, and budget apportionments.

If server resources are reduced see **OAT-015 Denial of Service** instead. Like **OAT-005 Scalping**, Denial of Inventory also reduces the availability of goods or services.

Other Names and Terms

Hoarding; Hold all attack; Inventory depletion; Inventory exhaustion; Stock exhaustion

See Also

- OAT-005 Scalping
- OAT-013 Sniping
- OAT-015 Denial of Service

CAPEC Category / Attack Pattern IDs

- 210 Abuse of Functionality

WASC Threat IDs

- 21 Insufficient Anti-Automation
- 42 Abuse of Functionality

CWEs

- 799 Improper Control of Interaction Frequency
- 841 Improper Enforcement of Behavioral Workflow

OWASP Attacks

- Abuse of Functionality

v1.2

OWASP Automated Threat Handbook Web Applications

Denial of Inventory   OAT-021

Deplete goods or services stock without ever completing the purchase or committing to the transaction.

Possible Symptoms
- Inventory balances reduce quickly
- Increased stock held in baskets or reservations
- Elevated basket abandonment
- Reduced use of payment step
- Increasing complaints from users being unable to obtain goods/services

Suggested Threat-Specific Countermeasures

Class	Threat-Specific Comments
Value	Consider requiring a deposit to reserve or book the goods/services. Consider providing incentives for quicker progression through checkout to payment.
Requirements	Document allocation/assignment policies and related settings/rules for identified applicable capacities and time outs. Consider how settings/limits should vary for seasonal or time-limited or low-availability stock.
Testing	Define test cases for **OAT-021 Denial of Inventory** that confirm the application will detect and/or prevent users attempting to remove inventory/stock from availability and hold onto it without paying/completing.
Capacity	Not applicable
Obfuscation	Consider randomising the content and URLs of product/catalogue pages and addition to basket/assignment processes.
Fingerprinting	Consider identifying and restricting automated usage by fingerprinting the User Agent for its unique characteristics.
Reputation	Consider identifying and restricting automated usage by reputational methods.
Authentication	Consider requiring greater identity authentication before goods/services can be allocated/assigned. Empty all items from baskets of anonymous users when their session expires.
Rate	Inform users of item holding time-outs. Consider limiting individual basket capacities. Consider increasing basket and basket item time-outs, or making these dynamic in response to demand and/or expiration dates. Consider reducing the time period reservation allocations remain valid. Consider disabling cash purchases for goods/services at certain times. Consider moving older baskets to wish lists. Consider limiting addition/re-addition to basket/allocation/assignment mechanisms per user, per group of users, per IP address/range, per device ID/fingerprint etc.
Monitoring	Log inventory allocation and de-allocation for each good/service item, log per session allocation, individually and in aggregate, across all channels (web, mobile app, call centre, physical retail stores, etc). Log drop-out rates for reservation/click & collect/pay by cash services. Identify stock issues raised by customers/clients/citizens; monitor trends.
Instrumentation	Consider emptying or disabling baskets etc in a particular session, IP address range or geolocation once Monitoring has identified a real Denial of Inventory attack, or other anomalous behaviour that has identified the user as an attacker
Contract	Define T&Cs to explicitly ban users from using the application in a way that leads to denial of inventory. Use contracts to prohibit employees and partners from undertaking or instigating such attacks against competitors.
Response	Define actions to be taken in the event a Denial of Inventory attack is detected.
Sharing	Participate in threat intelligence exchanges.

Printed in the USA
CPSIA information can be obtained
at www.ICGtesting.com
LVHW070812091123
763293LV00031B/9